Between Author and Editor

Exceptional Collaborations
During the Golden Age of American Book Publishing

Also by Thomas Fensch ...

Steinbeck and Covici:
    The Story of a Friendship
Conversations with John Steinbeck
The FBI files on Steinbeck
Essential Elements of Steinbeck
Steinbeck's bitter fruit:
    from The The Grapes of Wrath to Occupy Wall Street
The Man Who Was Dr. Seuss;
    The Life and Work of Theodor Geisel
Of Sneetches and Whos and the Good Dr. Seuss:
    Essays on the Life and Work of Theodor Geisel
The Man Who Was Walter Mitty:
    The Life and Work of James Thurber:
Conversations with James Thurber
The Man Who Changed His Skin:
    The Life and Work of John Howard Griffin
Behind Islands in the Stream:
    Hemingway; Cuba, the FBI and the crook factory
Oskar Schindler and His List:
    The Man, the Book, the Film, the Holocaust and Its Survivors
Foreshadowing Trump:
    Trump characters, Ethics, Morality and Fascism in Classic Literature
Timeless (Pen) Names:
    The Life and Work of Charles Lutwidge Dodgson, Samuel Langhorne Clemens, Eric Blair and Theodor Geisel
The Kennedy-Khrushchev Letters
Orwell in America
The Books That Haunt Us
Masters of Despair
Anne & Emmett:
    The tragic deaths and enduring legacies of Anne Frank and Emmett Till

... and others ...

BETWEEN AUTHOR
AND EDITOR

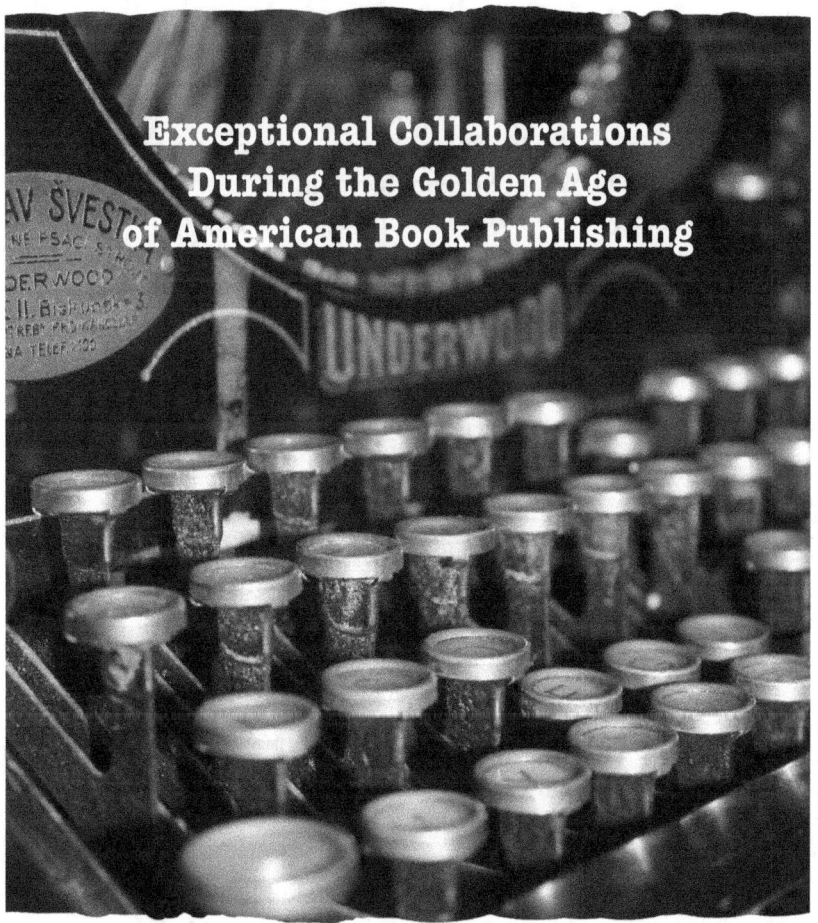

Exceptional Collaborations
During the Golden Age
of American Book Publishing

Thomas Fensch

Between Author and Editor

Copyright © 2024 Thomas Fensch All rights reserved. No part of this book may be reproduced or utilized by any form, or by any means, electronic or mechanical, including photocopying, recording, or by any information storage or retrieval system without written permission of the publisher.

New Century Books
Publishing trade books and ebooks since January, 2000
8821 Rockdale Rd.
N. Chesterfield, Va., 23236
newcentbks@gmail.com

ISBN: 979-8-9888347-2-4 (paperback)
ISBN: 979-8-9888347-5-5 (ebook)

Book design by Jill Ronsley, suneditwrite.com
Cover image courtesy of Pixabay

Chapter One—appeared in very, very abbreviated form—and material on John Steinbeck and Pascal Covici originally appeared in:
Steinbeck and Covici: The Story of a Friendship
Middlebury, Vt: Paul S. Eriksson, Publisher, 1979
Reprint ed., New Century Books, 2002

Contents

Introduction
i

Chapter 1
The Best of Times, The Worst of Times:
The author-editor relationship
1

Chapter 1—Notes
68

Chapter 2
"You are my rarest experience ..."
75

Chapter 2—Notes
128

Index
137

Bibliography
147

About the Author
151

Introduction

Was there ever a Golden Age in American book publishing?

We could consider the years from the mid-30s through the end of World War Two—or slightly more than that—the golden years; a cadre of editors and publishers—a good ol' boys network solely in New York City—where everyone knew everyone else.

Is that still the case? Surely not. Book publishing, which had previously been the lowest of the media industries in terms of revenue, is now huge business.

In her web article, "The 15 Largest Publishing Companies in the World," Caitlin Mazur delineates the top companies.

The top ten are:

- Pearson Education: a British-based company, which has revenue, of 4.751 billion and has a variety of imprints including Prentice-Hall, Longman, and others. Their sales are global, but 60 percent of sales comes from the United States;
- Penguin Random House: US. based—formed by the merger of Random House, owned by the German media conglomerate Bertlesmann and Penguin Group, owned by Pearson. Annual revenue: 4.09 billion. It publishes 15,000 titles annually among 250 divisions;

- Hachette Group, France, revenue 2.748 billion;
- Harper Collins, USA, division of News Corp, 2.19 billion;
- John Wiley & Sons, USA, revenue 2.08 billion;
- Springer Nature, British-German company, 1.86 billion;
- Scholastic, USA, 1.64 billion;
- McGraw-Hill, USA, 1.54 billion;
- Kodansha, Japanese, 1.48 billion;
- Macmillan, British-based, 1.4 billion.

In 2022, Penguin Random House attempted to acquire Simon & Schuster in a deal that would have cost Penguin Random House 2.175 billion. The U.S. Department of Justice sued to stop the acquisition on the grounds that it would create not a monopoly but a monopsony, or too much control over suppliers; i.e. top-selling writers.

The case was held before Federal Judge Florence Pan, in the United States District Court for the District of Columbia; she sided with the government to block the acquisition.

The editors cited during the Golden Years of Book Publishing often referred to the Book-of-the-Month Club. During those years it was a key to distribution.

What happened? It ceased operations for a time, was reorganized, passed through several owners and was re-introduced in 2015. It now claims to have 100,000 active member/subscribers.

Taking its place now is Amazon, which was established in the 1990s by Jeff Bezos originally to sell books. It has a near monopoly and controls 80 percent of book distribution in the United States. In the past it has dictated terms and conditions/controls on the wholesale prices of books; i.e. publishers had to accept Amazon's terms, or not get distribution through Amazon.

Unless there is some sort of federal intervention, that near monopoly is likely to continue.

An aspiring or novice author may rightly assume that the chances of attracting the attention of an editor at one of these mega-publishing firms—an editor who would shepherd a book by a novice writer through the publishing process—would be slim to none. (Old joke: "the odds are slim to none and Slim's outta town.")

The answer today is *print-on-demand*—*POD*—publishing. This book is a POD book.

This is the process for this book: once the entire manuscript is completed, a paper copy is sent to Bound Book Scanning, outside New York City. They scan the manuscript into one computer file, quickly and inexpensively. The file is then sent as an e-mail attachment to Ms. Jill Ronsley at Suneditwrite.com

She does the pagination and formats the interior of the book. She and the author collaborate on the front cover and back cover text. All versions, hardcover, paperback and e-book versions of the book (in this case paperback only) need individual ISBN numbers (International Standard Book Numbers) for the copyright page. (Their own license plates, so to speak.)

Once Ms. Ronsley has completed the interior file and the cover file, they are sent to Lightning Source, outside Nashville by "drag and drop." (The files can be simply pulled across the computer screen into the correct slots on the Lightning Source web page.) The author can supply the ISBN numbers or Lightning Source can supply them.

Once Lightning Source has verified that the metadata files match their criteria (Ms. Ronsley's files *always* match the Lightning Source computer system perfectly), they can be "up" as a book on Amazon within 48 hours.

The printing process with old-fashioned steps used to take up to one full year. (A few books even went out-of-date during the year before they were printed.) POD technology changes this to a few weeks—at most. Books are then printed *only after orders come in*. Print *on Demand*. There is never any overstock—the kinds of unsold books that appear later in the dollar stores and other such outlets. There are never huge piles of books in a publisher's warehouse. These files exist in Lightning Source's "Digital Library."

And, as an extra advantage—if a typo does appear in the text or the cover, a new file with a correction can simply be substituted—sent to Lightning Source.

And, as an additional advantage—traditional publishers pay author royalties once a year or—if the author is lucky—twice a year.

Lightning Source pays its publishing partners *every month* (after a usual three months accounting process; i.e. sales in January of any year are paid in early May, and so on for each subsequent month.)

Lightning Source has printed over 5,000,000 books with this technology. And they also publish ebooks, based on the same files.

This is the future of book publishing.

Finally, the author-publisher relationship: one of the most enduring collaborations was that of John Steinbeck and Pascal Covici.

Covici read John Steinbeck's first three books, which were published by three different firms that went bankrupt during the Great Depression; Covici then wanted to publish Steinbeck.

He published Steinbeck's subsequent books, first at his own firm Covici-Friede, then at The Viking Press. Steinbeck could have gone, as author, to firm A, then move to firm B, then to firm C after the success of *The Grapes of Wrath*, but he stayed with Covici for the rest of his career, broken only by Covici's death.

Their story is summarized in this book. A full analysis of their relationship appears in *Steinbeck and Covici: The Story of a Friendship*, first published in 1979 and reprinted in 2002. That book has long been considered a seminal work on Steinbeck scholarship.

And ... enter Dr. Seuss, a.k.a. Theodor Geisel. His first publication was the illustrations for *Boners*, 1931, a collection of humorous schoolyard gaffes. His own first real book was *And to Think That I Saw it on Mulberry Street*, 1937. Mulberry Street was a real street in his hometown of Springfield, Mass. He followed that with *The 500 Hats of Bartholomew Cubbins*, 1938, both published by the Vanguard Press, New York. At the same time, Bennett Cerf was building his relatively-new firm Random House and concentrating on adult titles. Cerf's wife suggested he establish a children's literature section at Random House.

Cerf knew of Geisel's books at Vanguard Press, but Geisel was legally obligated to Vanguard for his next one, or perhaps more, titles.

What to do?

Cerf simply bought the Vanguard Press and merged all its titles into Random House, thus obtaining Geisel.

Geisel's first two books for Random House were *The King's Stilts*, 1938, and *The Seven Lady Godivas*, 1939, a retelling of the Lady Godiva folklore tale.

There were nudes in Geisel's *Godivas*, they were loopy and mal-formed and not at all sexy, but librarians wanted no part of nudes *in any form* in their *kiddie lit* sections. The book was then a financial disaster, but these days a collector's item for Seuss lovers.

Bennett Cerf may have thought: *What have we done? Buying The Vanguard Press only to publish this disaster...*

But eventually Cerf's purchase of The Vanguard Press was redeemed: 16 books by Dr. Seuss have been listed in the all-time best-selling children's books, including *Green Eggs and Ham* at number 4; *The Cat in the Hat* at number 9; and *One Fish, Two Fish, Red Fish, Blue Fish* at number 13.

In fact, Random House income from the Dr. Seuss titles could—by themselves—finance a small(er) publishing house.

And what of his pen-name? His pseudonym? Seuss was Geisel's mother's maiden name. In German it would have been pronounced *Zoyce*, but no one knew that and no matter. Geisel had planned to use his own name for an adult title, but that never materialized—from *The Man Who Was Dr. Seuss*.

He stayed with Random House his entire life.

Dr. Seuss books have been known and loved by generations of children—and adults—throughout the world.

—Thomas Fensch
N. Chesterfield, Va.
August, 2023

Chapter 1

THE BEST OF TIMES, THE WORST OF TIMES:
The Author-Editor Relationship

For an author, the act of writing a book-length manuscript and watching it progress through the publishing processes may be, to paraphrase Charles Dickens, the best of times, and the worst of times. It is the best of times, of course, because a creative intellect brought forth the book; the idea; the project; the germ of individuality. It may be the worst of times, because any number of actual or imagined tragedies may befall the project during the editing and design and publishing stages; the book, even after being completed in manuscript, may not ever reach the book-buying public at all. The author may feel that he is at the whim of a merciless editor and publisher. Even if the manuscript is accepted for publication by a reputable company, the manuscript may be edited by a reputable editor away from the direction the author wished it to take.

The author too may think that the design of the book itself, the printing, publication and distribution, and attendant advertising and promotion may cause the book to fail rather than succeed; he may believe that the editor and publisher are conspiring to hinder, rather than help his brain-child. For some authors, the act of publishing, whether in fiction or non-fiction, is the worst of times, either in actual fact or in their imagination.

Publishing never has been a process which can be calculated precisely, either in terms of sales of copies, or in terns of successful author-publisher-public relationships.

The publishing process, also, has not been conducive to scholarly analysis. There have been few attempts to analyze the characteristics of a popular book; rather, in the main, attempts to analyze the actual success of popular books have been quantitively, rather than qualitatively determined.

The noted historian of journalism Frank Luther Mott[1] attempted to place the popular book in perspective in his *Golden Multitudes*[2]. He notes that the achievement of a popular success is almost beyond categorization:

> What makes a best seller?
>
> This is the sixty-four dollar question. It can be answered, though largely by guess and surmise, and never satisfactorily to the inquirer, who always wants a formula. There is no formula which may be depended upon to produce a best seller.
>
> There are too many impalpable considerations, too many chances and accidents, too complex a combination of conditions affecting the writing, publication and selling of a book to make the attainment of the top rank by even the most promising candidate a certainty. The creation of a best seller does not follow an exact pattern, or patterns, any more than does the making of a successful man; there are too many intangibles, too many unmeasurable human values, too many vicissitudes of fortune involved. Moreover, since there is not just one best seller audience, no single formula could be expected

to provide books for a buying public which is, thank God, pretty hetergeneous after all.

But just as the biographer, the psychologist, or the sociologist may correlate cases in order to study the roots of human success, so may the student of best sellers analyze and classify his materials to learn more about what seems to have made books succeed. Many lines of investigation immediately present themselves, but only a few of the more obvious conclusions of such a study will be presented here. One cannot escape the almost constant appearance in all periods of our best seller history of certain elements of popular appeal—as religion, sensationalism, information and guidance, adventure, democracy, humor, characterization, juvenile suitability, timeliness, and so on.[3]

To simplify his study, Mott determined that a "best seller" was the sales figure of "one per cent of the total population of continental United States for the decade in"[4] which the book was published," which is as workable an arbitrary figure as any. Using that formula, Mott was then able to determine which books achieved that sales figure. He then was able to calculate which books, fiction and non-fiction, achieved "best sellerdom" during the literary history of this country.

When Bennett Cerf asked "What makes a book sell?" his answer was:

> That's a question that people have been arguing about since the publishing business started. Is it word of mouth? Is it fortuitous circumstances? Is it book club choice? Is it good publishing exploitation? Or is it advertising?

All the advertising in the world will not sell a book that has not gotten some kind of start for itself. Like a car stuck in the mud. If it is really stuck, 10 people can't get it started. But if it is moving just a little bit, one man can push it.... Of course, if you have a book by an author who is well known, you are in before you start. It doesn't require any great skill to make a best seller from a book by John O'Hara or James Michener or Truman Capote. The publisher who is worth his salt is the one who can take one unknown, find a handle for the book and put it over. That is the exciting part of publishing, discovering some new talent and watching the talent burst on the scene. Then watching the author change overnight.[5]

James D. Hart, the author and scholar, has suggested that:

Literary taste is not an isolated phenomenon. The taste of the largest number of readers is shaped by contemporary pressures more than is the taste of the highly cultivated reader, who has a deeper background of aesthetic experience and knowledge to guide him. Books flourish when they answer a need and die when they do not. The needs of the greatest reading public are various: They include clarification of ideas already in circulation; emotional statement of feelings that people are prepared to accept; popularization of desirable information heretofore obscure; satisfying appeal to forms of entertainment currently considered amusing or exciting. Ranged in this order, one might list as American examples Tom Paine's *The American Crisis*; Mrs. Stowe's *Uncle Tom's Cabin*; Will Durant's *The Story of Philosophy*; and

Erie Stanley Gardner's *The Case of the Curious Bride*. But none of these are popular only because it answered the need with which is here matched, and there are many books whose popularity relates to a most subtle blending of appeals to all these and other needs of the public.[6]

Hart suggests that it is often easy to determine why a book has succeeded; and it is often easy, in retrospect, to determine why a particular book failed. If the book in question was the first of its type, the initial novelty of the work may make it a great popular success. Similarly, the final book in a sequence (by the same publisher, or similar books on the same theme by different publishing houses), may become a success because the house or publishing houses in question paved the way for the success of the later work.[7]

He suggests, however, that the continued sustained work by one particular author cannot easily be estimated either, even when the work of the author has been published by the same firm. Advertising and promotion of subsequent titles may not help carry the first, or earlier titles to continued success. Quoting Hart:

> Some writers, like Scott or Dickens, make a reputation early, amass a loyal following and continue adding to it those persons who 'missed' the first books and want to read the later ones to enter the discussion that follows publication of a new work. On the other hand, there are authors like Pearl Buck, whose first book sells enormously and whose subsequent ones do less well, perhaps because the novelty of subject, point of view, or style wears off and, if necessary, the later books can be discussed in terms of the first.[8]

Robert Banker, assistant manager of the Doubleday bookstores, has suggested a litany of why book store buyers buy, or don't buy, selective titles from book salesmen, or travellers, as they are called in the trade. Banker suggests that gossip from one book traveller, about the potential success of a title may influence a book store clerk to order copies. "The bookseller is as prone to listen to gossip as any other member of the reading public," he suggests.[9]

The price, the dust jacket design or lack of it, the actual size and heft of the hardcover book in the purchaser's hands, and the advance advertising by the publisher in book trade magazines and in general circulation newspapers and magazines all contribute to the potential success of placing the book in the retail clerk's hands and aiding him in selling it to the book-buying public which comes into the bookstore.[10]

The existence of the mail-order book club, a relatively recent phenomenon in the publishing business, has been seen generally as a good adjunct to the successful bookstore sale of trade books, as mail sales to subscription patrons of the book club eventually meant increased sales by bookstores to the same individuals. As Harold Latham, a Macmillan editor wrote, the advent of the Book-of-the-Month Club and other similar ventures has advantages and disadvantages, in equal measure:

> The Book-of-the-Month Club promised to be a new means of distribution. With wide circularization and tempting offers, it did invade areas barren of bookstores and added tens of thousands of names to its lists. It cannot be argued, it seems to me, that the effect of book clubs in catering to localities without bookstores, in bringing books to people, has been anything but

good. It has, I am sure, greatly added to the body of book readers by making books easier to get.

In this respect, then, the Book-of-the-Month Club has kept to one of its first purposes ... (but) it has seemed to me that it has sometimes surrendered to the demands of popular taste....

Someone has said that we no longer have real best sellers made so by actual book readers; that what we have are artificial best sellers, selected by a board of editors and foisted on the public by them. This is in a measure true, though not so true now ... as it was a few years back.[11]

In summary, Frank Luther Mott wrote:

> But finally, after recounting all that a publisher can do for a book, by way of employing all the old and proven methods and devising new and experimental techniques, we have to admit that his success in any given case is very uncertain.... Nobody can be sure—neither the inspired author nor the Inspired publisher—of the precise combination which will bring the tremendous response necessary to make a best seller. It is a tricky business, full of chances, timely and untimely strokes of fortune, lucky hits and unexplainable lapses....[12]

But these are not the only factors in successful publishing. The focus of the rest of this chapter, and indeed the rest of this book, will be to demonstrate that one of the heretofore indefinable facets of successful publishing is the relationship of the author and the editor, during the publishing process. The bond—acceptance by the editor of the author's work—and acceptance by the author of the editor's judgment—is an ethereal one at best. The author-editor relationship has existed in a variety of successful and unsuccessful forms and styles during the course of recent American publishing. The remainder of this chapter will cite examples of the relationship as it has existed and how the relationship eventually helped mold the author's completed manuscript.

Of this author-editor relationship, Cass Canfield, the Harper's editor and publisher, has written:

> The editor stands or falls on his ability to persuade his authors to accept the changes and revisions he proposes to the author or makes himself. Again and again, particularly when an editor lacks tact, the author will leave him and seek a more sympathetic publisher. In many such cases he will eventually make the very changes proposed by the first editor; when this happens, the original editor may derive some melancholy satisfaction from having helped to improve a manuscript, even though in the process he lost an author.
>
> How does a good editor edit? He does this by attempting to persuade the author to revise his manuscript. That is the secret, for the author knows more about his book than anyone else. The editor can make intelligent suggestions, but, when these are not carried out, the editor must get to work on the manuscript himself and put it into shape. He must strive to see the book as a whole and show the author how to make changes in the beginning, middle or end of his manuscript that will make it a more effective piece of writing.[13]

Regrettably for those editors who hold these views—that an editor *must* convince authors to make changes—there are times when the author in question simply will not make the editorial or stylistic changes which the editor believes is in the author's own best interest.

Canfield, himself, reached this point during his long association with Edna St. Vincent Millay. As he writes:

> Edna St. Vincent Millay was one of the most extraordinary people I have ever known, combining a beautiful lyrical gift with the mind of a mathematician. She was professional to her finger tips, and took justified pride in the technical perfection of manuscripts she sent to us, her publishers. Although I should have known better, I once questioned her use of a classical phrase. Then all hell broke loose....[14]

In her first letter to Cass Canfield about this matter she wrote:

> Dear Cass Canfield:
> It occurs to me with something of dismay, that, if I were dead—instead of being, as I am, alive and kicking, and I said kicking—the firm of Harper & Brothers (Est 1817—and how good is your Latin?) might conceivably, acting upon the advice of a cultured friend, alter one word of my poems.
> This you must never do. Any changes which might profitably be made in any of my poems, were either made by me, before I permitted them to be published, or must be made, if made at all, someday by me. Only

I, who know what I mean to say, and how I want to say it, am competent to deal with such matters. Many of my poems, of course, are greatly reduced in stature from the majesty which I hoped they might achieve, because I was unable, as one too often is to make the poem rise up to my conception of it. However, the faults as well as the virtues of this poetry, are my own; and no other person, could possibly lay hands upon any poem of mine in order to correct some real or imagined error without harming the poem more seriously than any faulty execution of my own could possibly have done. (I do not, of course include here such hastily-written and hot-headed pieces as are contained in "Make Bright the Arrows," "The Murder of Lidice," etc. I am speaking of poetry composed with no other design than that of making as good a poem as one possibly can make, of poetry written with deliberation and under the sharp eye of an ever-alert self-criticism, of poetry, in other words, written with no ulterior motive such as, for instance, the winning of a world-war to keep democracy alive.)

As for sonnet XIV from "Epitaph for the Race of Man," let me assume you know (because I know that you are deeply troubled about this matter and in a mood to accept from a friend whose learning you respect, a suggested alternative in one of my poems) let me assure you that your friend has brashly leaped to an ill-considered conclusion, and that in this instance he has made a complete ass of himself.

This particular sonnet is guilty of a serious fault, but from the point of view of sonnet-structure, not from the point of view of either fact or mythology. The octave is written in the pure Italian form, whereas in the sonnet the rhyme-scheme (acul) is improper. This is very bad, of course. Yet I do consider this particular bastard sonnet to be sometimes as in this sonnet, for instance, not ineffective.

As to what the sonnet actually <u>says</u>,—well, it seems to me that any bright boy in the eighth grade, who cared for poetry, and was not too lazy to look up a few words in the dictionary, would have little difaculty as to its literal meaning. If this poem makes any statement at all, which it does, than the substitution of the word "Ixion" for the word "Aeolus" would render the whole sonnet utterly ridiculous, confusing and meaningless....

I would not, if I were you, in the future, pay much attention to any suggestion made to you by this acquaintance of yours on the subject of poetry, for which, it would seem, he really cares very little, and concerning which, even more seriously, he knows even less. He is not, in any case, a thorough going student; he is a pouncer upon details and his scholarship—if indeed it exists at all—is bumpy and uneven.

Sincerely yours, and with every good wish for the New Year,

Edna St. Vincent Millay
January 8th, 1946.[15]

After "an avalanche of letters," Canfield notes, "I caved in, properly chastised."[16]

Such editor-author confrontations are decidedly not unusual, although they may take different forms and arguments. Certainly the relationship between Ring Lardner and his editor,

Maxwell Perkins of Charles Scribner's Sons, exhibits many of the same problems. Perkins was always uniformly courteous and reserved with Lardner—and he often met with frustration.

Perkins, of course, was an extremely perceptive editor. As Clifford M. Caruthers writes:

> Perkins was flexible enough to assume different roles with different writers. To Thomas Wolfe, from whose voluminous manuscripts Perkins extracted the published novels, Perkins became not only the close friend and advisor Wolfe needed (he was, later, even Wolfe's literary executor) but also virtually a coauthor, to the extent that Wolfe eventually switched to Harper & Bros. in a desperate effort to prove to the world that he could write his own novels. To Hemingway, Perkins astutely demonstrated his respect for the Hemingway mystique of the big game hunter and general sportsman. To (F. Scott) Fitzgerald, Perkins was, … not only a perceptive editor but also a personal advisor, friend and paternal figure for the sensitive, unstable Fitzgerald.[17]

Perkins' enthusiasm for Ring Lardner's work must have been severely tested. Perkins discovered that Lardner considered himself primarily a newspaper journalist and exhibited only a remote interest in having his short stories collected and published by Scribner's. Maxwell Perkins discovered, to his surprise, that Lardner did not even keep copies of his own published stories; Perkins and his office staff had to search through the back files of the New York Public Library for magazines such as the *Saturday Evening Post, Cosmopolitan, McClure's* and other general magazines. Perkins had to recopy Lardner's stories before they could be reset in type and printed in book form.

In viewing the extant Lardner-Perkins correspondence, Carruthers suggests:

> It is clear from these letters that, after 1923, the motivating force behind the publication of Lardner's books was always Maxwell Perkins, who selected the contents from Lardner's magazine publications, suggested format, chapter and sometimes book titles, offered plots, at times even tactfully reworked the text, and always encouraged Lardner to write more fiction, and especially to write the novel Perkins thought he could do, but which Lardner for various reasons never got around to writing.[19]

Perkins' first letter to Ring Lardner contains all the tact and sincerity that Perkins was capable of.

July 2, 1923

Dear Mr. Lardner:

I read your story "The Golden Wedding" with huge enjoyment. Scott Fitzgerald recommended it to me and he also suggested that you might have other material of the same sort, which, with this, could form a volume. I am therefore writing to tell you how very much interested we should be to consider this possibility, if you could put the material before us.

I would hardly have ventured to do this if Scott had not spoken of the possibility, because your position in the literary world is such that you must be besieged by publishers, and to people in that situation their letters of interest are rather a nuisance. I am certainly mighty glad to have the chance of expressing our interest though, if, as Scott thought, you would not feel that we were merely bothering you. Would you be willing to send on any material that might go with "The Golden Wedding" to form a volume, or to tell me where I might come at it in periodicals?

Very truly yours,[20]

Carruthers notes that it took Lardner five months to reply to Perkins, at a time when Perkins was publishing Hemingway, F. Scott Fitzgerald, Thomas Wolfe and others and was generally regarded as one of the most extraordinary editors in one of the major publishing houses in the country. Lardner is not likely to have ignored Perkins' importance—he and F. Scott Fitzgerald were great friends, and Fitzgerald, who told Perkins about the possibilities of publishing Lardner, must have advised Lardner of Perkins' expertise.

Thereafter, Perkins' letters reveal how he had to work to find Lardner's published material and the pains he took to edit and prepare Lardner's material for publication.

Dec. 7, 1923

Dear Mr. Lardner:

Thanks for the copy of "The Champion." I am glad to get it at last. I had tried advertising and everything else;—but I did find in the end that there was one other copy, H. L. Mencken's.

Now I have all the stories you spoke of that eventful evening when Scott drove into the lake. What an excellent sport he is about the failure of "The Vegetable"!

Sincerely yours,[21]

Perkins continued to have more and more difficulty in editing and even obtaining material for the Lardner books which he, Perkins, planned to release. The following notes how he even planned a book by Lardner without letting Lardner know (or asking his permission) when he would release it. Presumably Perkins felt that Lardner[1]'s approval would be automatic and he needn't bother his reluctant author with such matters:

Feb. 1, 1924

Dear Mr. Lardner:

I hope Scott has told you that we have actually gone so far as to put your "How To Write Short Stories" into the spring list:—a rather irregular proceeding since you have never told us we could. But we were very much interested in the general idea and we felt that the best thing to do was to act immediately and get out a volume. If this seems right to you, we will pay a fifteen percent royalty from the start on the first book.

I am having a bad time getting together the stories though. I have a letter from McClure's saying that they haven't got the issue for August 1915, and the Post did not have any story in the issue of December 6, 1919. I sent Scott a list of the stories that the Cosmopolitan had and will copy for us. I can have the Post looked through in the library between 1914 and 1919—for after that the Post is indexed—and see what we find and I think we can arrange to have the stories copied out. We will do the same with McClure's for August 1915. If we get these stories we will have a good representative collection.

Sincerely yours,[23]

One of Maxwell Perkins' next letters indicates how thoroughly he planned and designed Lardner's books:

Feb. 18, 1924

Dear Mr. Lardner:

Although I am notified by the Post that "Horseshoes" is on the way, I am not waiting for it, but am putting all the other stories in hand, in the following order:

How to Write Short Stories The Facts
Some Like 'Em Cold
Alibi Ike
Golden Honeymoon
Champion
My Roomy
A Caddy's Diary
A Frame-up
Harmony

You may not like this order, but it can easily be changed in the galleys. I considered first more or less grouping the stories but gave up the idea and went in the other direction:—that is, I aimed at variety. I thought that the several baseball stories ought to be scattered throughout the volume, for instance. The question of the first story was a hard one, but it could not be "The Golden Honeymoon" because that had appeared in the "Short Stories of 1922" volume. I did not think it ought to be a baseball story anyhow, because we want to place the emphasis differently in this whole scheme. I finally hit upon "The Facts" because it will please everybody, male and female, of every sort. Then I followed with "Some Like 'Em Cold" because it seemed to me to be a masterpiece in that sort of writing. At this point it seemed well to get in one of the baseball stories and "Alibi Ike" is a corker. I am sorry "Champion" comes so late in a way, but publishers probably exaggerate the importance of an early position. People don't begin at the beginning and read a book of stories straight through. The stories that follow I have arranged on the principle of variety.

I have been very anxious to get this book into the actual process of manufacture, but as soon as the proofs begin to come up, I will try to get you to let me take up with you the question of the earlier books,[24] and the plan of gathering them in from the publishers.

Sincerely yours,[25]

Thereafter, in Carruthers' words, "the correspondence that follows is the record of a highly personable and persuasive editor skillfully cajoling an amazingly reluctant author into cooperating in the collection of a substantial amount of memorable fiction." Lardner died in 1933, never having completed the long novel which Perkins was always urging him to write. Despite Lardner's alcoholism, his output was doubtlessly much higher than it would have been without Perkins' encouragement, help and advice, Carruthers believes.[26]

The observation that Perkins not only "suggested format, chapter and sometimes book titles,"[27] is not unique to Perkins and his relationship to Ring Lardner. Charles A. Madison, former editor at the Henry Holt Company (now Holt, Rinehart and Winston) notes that the same experience occurred to Sherwood Anderson.

Early in his career, a collection of Anderson's short stories was sent throughout the New York literary establishment, and uniformly rejected, until it reached the one-man office of editor and publisher B. W. Huebsch.

Huebsch liked the manuscript and published it only because he liked it, not because he thought it would make money for his firm. Huebsch also supplied the title for the collection; *Winesburg, Ohio*.[28]

Anderson's analysis of why he stayed with Huebsch indicates that although he could see flaws and faults in Huebsch's personality and business dealings, Anderson decided to stay with Huebsch for personal reasons rather than turn to a different editor/publisher for purely financial reasons. In October, 1921, Anderson wrote to Trigant Burrow, a personal friend:

> Let me say a few things to you about him (Huebsch). He really at bottom, I suspect, doesn't know what a good book is or how to sell books, but he is a fine fellow; and at any rate you wouldn't have to, with him, go through the wearisome business of having some smart publisher tell you what to do to make your book sell. There is somewhere hidden away in Benny a real altruistic streak. In practice it takes itself out in the Freeman. Besides which he is a single-taxer, a Socialist, and I'm not sure what else.
>
> As you know, my own books do not sell much, but I suppose a smart publisher could sell twice as many; at least several have come to me with the proposition that they would undertake to do something like that if I would only come to them. I've stuck with Ben because my years as a businessman cured me effectually of any desire to make money that there is almost a satisfaction in some of Ben's inefficiencies as a publisher. You will know what I mean by that.[29]

Earlier, Anderson wrote to Huebsch, explaining why he decided to stay with Huebsch:

> I am glad you like Winesburg. From the first I have had a hunch that you are the man I want to publish my stuff. It is so delightful to have a publisher you can have as a real friend also. I hope the stuff goes. I shall try to put something real in it.[30]

Two years later, Anderson again wrote of why he liked Huebsch, in a letter to Roger Sergei, another friend:

> As for Huebsch, one of the most sincere, lovable men I have ever known, God bless him. Behind the door I would whisper to you that I do not think too much of his artistic perception. He's a queer kind, had ideas, etc. ... and declare it to be an artistic masterpiece; and all the time you grow more and more to love him and respect him and to realize you would rather have him as your publisher selling 5,000 than some of the damned smart young men of the publishing world 'putting you over' to the tune of 25,000.[31]

Anderson began publishing with Huebsch in 1918; by 1921, financial matters had driven Anderson into believing that Huebsch might be cheating him. When Huebsch allowed The Modern Library to reprint *Winesburg, Ohio* in a reprint edition, Huebsch paid Anderson one half of the profits from that transaction, a figure which Anderson resented. Huebsch patiently explained that dividing a reprint check in half was a standard practice, but if Anderson wished, they could negotiate the matter:

I do not want to take up here the question of what seems to be a general practice, but I am ready to talk it over with you, with a view to modifying our contract, if it seems mutually fair to do so. I do not want to take advantage of merely technical rights. But I do ask, and most earnestly, that you attempt to disabuse the minds of those who carried away a wrong impression of my methods, because you know how easily a man's reputation can get a black eye.[32]

Madison writes that Anderson was not fully mollified by Huebsch's explanation, even though Huebsch was correct and ethical in his business arrangements.[33]

By late 1924, however, Anderson decided to accept an offer from another publisher, Horace Liveright; Liveright would advance him one hundred dollars a week for five years. Liveright's house would publish anything which Anderson completed during that time and the weekly payments would be deducted against the earned royalties of the Liveright-published materials.[34] Horace Liveright, always known as a gambler, gambled correctly. Anderson's next book, *Dark Laughter*, the first under the Liveright imprint, became a best seller for a time and sales eventually reached a total of 100,000 hardcover copies.[35] Thereafter, however, all of Anderson's other books under the Liveright imprint sold substantially less.

Anderson's sadness at leaving B. W. Huebsch, whom he genuinely admired, was contrasted with the (at least) temporary security that better sales brought, via the Liveright imprint. He wrote the following letter to Liveright, some months after their agreement was completed:

New Orleans
November 22, 1924

Dear Horace:

I have not wired you, because it will take nothing less than a letter to tell you how matters are with me, and I will have to answer your letter to you as a person rather than as a businessman and publisher. Last year when I was up against (it) and wanted a decent offer from someone, you made it to me without hesitation.

Otto[36] is one of my valued friends and has surely done a lot for me. I want to make everything as clear as I can. It may be you will feel I'm a fool.

The truth is I would just find it too hard and uncomfortable for me to make a change. When I started to do it last year, I felt like a dog. I wanted to do it and at the same time I didn't want to. While the negotiations were on, I felt like hell. I know, Horace, that all you say is probably correct. It takes an organization to place books, and if they aren't placed, they won't be sold. The number of people who will go out of their way to get books when they must be ordered from a distance or who will wait until a dealer gets them is small and always will be. All of these things I know and have known for a long time. Why, they haven't got *A Story Teller's Story* in the bookstore down here yet. (It) probably never will sell much.

On the other hand, Horace, I got out of business some years ago. Things like sticking to old friends have really got bigger to me than anything else. While Ben never has sold my books much, he has been very, very fine with me in other ways. There never has been any lack of moral support. He published me and gave me his support when no one else much wanted me.

At the same time, Horace, I think it is fine of you to want to give me this chance. There is no question of your not doing the right thing by Ben. It was me who opened the ball with you, but, really, I guess in doing so I wasn't quite myself. I got scared about money matters, … Usually I'm not scared about making a living. I do it always after a fashion. And from now on I am likely to do more and, I hope, better work than I have done before.[37]

Anderson and Liveright remained on good terms, although Anderson later cancelled the one hundred dollar-per week advance because it weighed too heavily on his mind. Liveright's publishing firm collapsed in the crash of 1929, and, in 1933, Anderson began publishing with Maxwell E. Perkins, and the Charles Scribner firm. In an early letter to Perkins, Anderson speaks of the ideal author-publisher relationship; he terms it "a kind of intellectual marriage":

August 10, 1933

Dear Maxwell Perkins;

I like your letter about my coming with Scribner's and I know you must know that I decided to come with your house, not because of any advance you might give me on a particular book, any amount of advertising of my books you might do, etc., but because of a genuine respect I have long had for the position of the house of Scribner's in the publishing world, and also, may I say, because I instinctively liked you, Mr. Perkins.

I do think, however, Mr. Perkins, that there is something in your letter of which I think I should speak. You say that the first book to be put out by your house must be either a novel or a continuous narrative, something after the manner of *A Story Teller's Story*, and in this I think you are right. I know that I myself spoke of this later book. I am calling it tentatively *I Build My House*.[38] It is a book I have long wanted to write. In fact, when I came home from New York last week, having the play temporarily off my hands, I immediately plunged into it. The general plan of the book is a story of my own experiences in the American literary world, people met, what has hurt and what has helped me in my own particular effort to produce beautiful literature here.

I want to write this book now and expect to devote myself to it, but I do think there might be exceptions taken to what seems somewhat a too strong pronouncement. I do not believe you mean it so.

I think I should feel free to come to you from time to time and talk of plans as to a friend. I have a certain conception of what I conceive to be the right relationship between a writer and publisher, a relationship that might be, at its best, a kind of intellectual marriage, and in any such relationship I do not think that either side should be too positive.

I say all of this with no intention of trying to get you to publish anything of mine ahead of the sort of more important things you speak of, but rather to put down a kind of general feeling I have and that I think should at once be made as clear as possible. am sure you will agree with me.

        Sincerely,[39]

Anderson remained on generally good terms with Perkins until Anderson died in 1942. Earlier, in a letter to Perkins, he indicated how he felt toward his various editors and publishers, and suggested that the book on which he was then working (which eventually was published as *Sherwood Anderson's Memoirs*) would need greater promotion than was ever given to his earlier works.

August 16, 1940

Dear Max:

Your letter touched me. It had in it the note I have always felt in you and liked in you.

At the same time, Max, I can't live by merely being thought of as a sometime master of my craft.

It is, Max, my own pretty firm belief that the American people do not buy books. Books are sold to them. Pretty much everything is sold to Americans.

When I began publishing, I began with Ben Huebsch, who had a curious reluctance about selling books. I stayed with him a long time, for years. I was, at the time, strong enough to work, often at work I hated, to make a living and support my children and do my writing at night. I had finally to quit him or starve.

I went to Horace Liveright, and while he lived, Horace did sell my books. He took a gamble on me, and he won and I won. Horace had, as we both know, a lot of unpleasant things about him, but he did put a roof over my head and free me from having to sit day after day in a damn advertising office.

Which convinced me that my books could be sold.

I think it takes a personal interest, a willingness to gamble a little on me, go back of my books.

I had a feeling. Max, when I went to Scribner's that I might get this kind of interest. I have a suspicion that perhaps I didn't get it because Mr. Scribner thought of me as a man too old to spend money on.

I understand that. It was all right with me, but I did, frankly, expect a better job of selling my books than I got.

And I know from experience that it can be done.

And I haven't really blamed you, Max. I just figured your real interest was in other men.

It may take a long time, a year or two, tc get down all I want to put down in this book on which I am now at work. I have had pretty damn good offers on it. I think I can make it an important book that can be sold by a house that is willing to go back of it.

I don't believe you can blame me for feeling as I do, Max.

Whatever I do, I want you as a friend.

Sincerely,[40]

Even more than his relationship with Anderson, Maxwell E. Perkins is known by his close association with two other novelists, Thomas Wolfe and F. Scott Fitzgerald, although Perkins was the editor and publisher for a great many others, including Ernest Hemingway and Ring Lardner.

Thomas Wolfe, born in Asheville, North Carolina, in 1900, began writing while attending the University of North Carolina. After graduation, he began teaching at New York University, and saving to travel to Europe. After a year in Europe, in 1925, he returned with the uncompleted first draft of a manuscript he tentatively titled either *O Lost* or *Alone, Alone*.[41]

The firm of Boni & Liveright received the manuscript first and promptly rejected it. Aline Bernstein, Wolfe's friend, then sent it to Harcourt, Brace and Co., which also rejected it. Pascal Covici's firm of Covici-Friede then read the manuscript and also rejected it, but did ask for an option on Wolfe's second (and presumably more mature) work. Undaunted, one of Wolfe's friends sent the manuscript to the Scribner's firm, where a house reader first rejected it, then had second thoughts and sent it to Maxwell Perkins. The date of Perkins' reply was October 22, 1928 and he wrote Wolfe:

Dear Mr. Wolfe:

Mrs. Ernest Boyd left with us, some weeks ago, the manuscript of your novel, "0 Lost." I do not know whether it would be possible to work out a plan by which it might be worked into a form publishable by us, but I do know that, setting the practical aspects of the matter aside, it is a very remarkable thing, and that no editor could read it-without being excited by it and filled with admiration by many passages in it and sections of it.

Your letter, that came with it, shows you realize what difficulties it presents, so that I need not enlarge upon this side of the question.

What we should like to know is whether you will be in New York in a fairly near future, when we can see you and discuss the manuscript. We should certainly look forward to such an interview with very great interest.

Very truly yours,[42]

At that point, according to Andrew Turnbull, one of Wolfe's biographers, Wolfe "was entering the orbit of one of the most remarkable men this nation has produced."

Turnbull wrote, of Perkins' methods:

> The influence of a great editor, like that of a teacher, is a subtle, atmospheric thing not easily defined, but with Perkins the root of it was his integrity. Meeting him, you knew right off that here was a man incapable of a cheap or shabby act and one you could trust forever. His respect for others followed naturally from his deep selfrespect (not to be confused with self-regard or conceit), and he gave his authors a sense of caring as much about their work as they did. Besides which, he had an uncanny knack of putting himself in their places and visualizing their problems from the inside, for Perkins was essentially an artist whose medium was the writing of other men. Like an artist, he entrusted his instincts and shied away from the prescribed or formularized, even to the point of discouraging advance summaries of novels lest they fetter the author's imagination.
>
> His criticism, as a rule so keen and unerring, was offered tentatively, obliquely, half-reluctantly; as one writer described it, asking Perkins for advice was like dropping pebbles down a well and listening for the splash. "Don't ever defer to my judgment," he wrote (F. Scott) Fitzgerald early in their relationship.[44]

There is no underestimating the influence that Perkins had on the emotional Wolfe. Perkins had a great influence, on Wolfe, initially observing that Wolfe's material could not be published in the huge chunks that Wolfe brought to Scribner's. Madison wrote:

Perkins went over the manuscript[45] with him to indicate general reorganization, the parts in need of revision, passages which might be omitted, and places which required additional material. Soon, however, he realized that Wolfe was unable to cut and revise as he had suggested. By now interested as much in the author as in the manuscript, he took over the process of detailed revision, explaining, cajoling, urging, directing.[46]

So it went. Perkins, with Wolfe's consent, reduced the manuscript about a third[47] before publication. By the time *Look Homeward, Angel* was published, Perkins had replaced Aline Bernstein as the prime focus of his life. In the words of Madison, "Perkins gradually replaced her as his (Wolfe's) surrogate parent, friend and confessor."[48] On the day before Christmas, 1929, Wolfe wrote to Perkins, expressing his affirmation of Perkins' aid:

> Harvard Club
> New York
> Dec. 24, 1929

Dear Mr. Perkins:

One year ago I had little hope for my work, and I did not know you. What has happened since may seem to be only a modest success to many people; but to me it is touched with strangeness and wonder. It is a miracle.

You are now mixed with my book in such a way that I can never separate the two of you. I can no longer think clearly of the time I wrote it, but rather of the time when you first talked to me about it, and when you worked upon it. My mind has always seen people more clearly than events or things—the name "Scribner's" naturally makes a warm glow in my heart but you are chiefly "Scribner's" to me: you have done what I had ceased to believe one person could do for another—you have created liberty and hope for me.

Young men sometimes believe in the existence of heroic figures, stronger and wiser than themselves, to whom they can turn for an answer to all their vexation and grief. Later, they must discover that such answers have to come out of their own hearts; but the powerful desire to believe in such figures persists. You are for me such a figure: you are one of the rocks to which my life is anchored.[49]

When Wolfe became despondent because of an unfavorable review, and told Perkins he was to write no more, Perkins told him:

If I really believed you would be able to stand by your decision, your letter would be a great blow to me. I cannot believe it, though. If anyone were ever destined to write, that one is you.[50]

Later, when Perkins saw Wolfe having trouble editing his own material, Perkins was almost as agonized as Wolfe. Perkins observed:

I, who thought Tom a man of genius, and loved him too, and could not bear to see him fail, was almost as desperate as he,—so much there was to do—But the truth is that if I did him a real service—and in this I did—it was keeping from losing his belief in himself in a crisis by believing in him. What he most needed was comradeship and understanding in a long crisis—these things I could give him then.[51]

When Wolfe's *Of Time and the River* was published, he dedicated it to Perkins.

Yet eventually, Wolfe's attitudes toward Perkins changed. When Scribner's published a small volume of Wolfe's, *The Story of a Novel*, Wolfe quarreled over the price and the size of the book.

During the same period, Bernard DeVoto, the critic and editor asserted that Wolfe could do no writing without the help of 'Mr. Perkins and the assembly-line at Scribner's,"[52] a criticism that stung Wolfe.

Perkins' letters to Wolfe from 1934 and 1937 indicate that Perkins was trying as best he could to placate and appease his volcanic author; and to keep him in the Scribner family, despite whatever costs to Perkins' dignity. His letters to Wolfe are, in the main, calm and reasoned, yet Wolfe could not or would not see that Perkins and Scribner's had acted fairly and decently toward him from the beginning of the relationship. The following letter to Wolfe from Perkins dated November 18, 1936, indicates Perkins' willingness to reason with Wolfe and keep him in the Scribner fold:

Nov. 18, 1936

Dear Tom:

With this is a more formal letter which I hope is what you want. This is to say that on my part there has been no "severance." I can't express certain kinds of feelings very comfortably, but you must realize what my feelings are toward you. Ever since *"Look Homeward,*

Angel" your work has been the foremost interest in my life, and I have never doubted for your future on any grounds except, at times, on those of your being able to control the vast mass of material you have accumulated and have to form into books. You seem to think I have tried to control you. I only did that when you asked my help and then I did the best I could. It all seems very confusing to me but, whatever the result, I hope you don't mean it to keep us from seeing each other, or that you won't come to our house.

Max[54]

Wolfe began negotiating with the publishing firm of Houghton, Mifflin and delivered a manuscript consisting of "a packing case and nine smaller containers."[53] When the firm asked Wolfe to sign a waiver of responsibility for the manuscript when it was in its offices, Wolfe refused in a huff, reclaimed the manuscript and ceased further negotiating with Houghton, Mifflin. The firm of Doubleday became interested in him, but Wolfe found a friend in Edward C. Aswell, of Harper and Bros. Aswell, like Wolfe, was a native southerner and Wolfe drew near to him because of that common bond. Wolfe signed with Harper's on the last day of 1937, yet wrote a warm, emotional letter to Charles Scribner:

> I think you are not only the finest publishers, but among the finest people I have ever known. Whatever comes of all this, I know we will be friends, and now that I am committed to a new, and for me, very lonely and formidable course, that knowledge gives me the deepest comfort.[56]

Early in 1938, he began his association with Harper's and Edward C. Aswell. Before they could begin extensive work, Wolfe felt the need to travel and toured the national parks in the west. While en route to Vancouver, Wolfe shared a drink with a stranger, caught the man's influenza and became deeply ill. Previously undiagnosed tuberculosis had remained in his system, and when he became ill, the disease traveled to his brain.

Thomas Wolfe died on September 15, 1938, leaving unfulfilled the relationship which meant so much to Maxwell Perkins. Aswell was able eventually to publish *The Web and the Rock*, *You Can't Go Home Again*, and *The Hills Beyond* under the Harper's imprint.

Yet, despite his late association with the publishing house of Harper, it is the relationship with Maxwell E. Perkins and the Scribner firm for which Wolfe and Perkins are remembered.[57]

Wolfe's last letter to Perkins, a little over a month before his death, indicates the depth of feeling and emotion he harbored for the man who first published him and believed in him.

> Providence Hospital
> Seattle, Washington
> August 12, 1938

Dear Max:

I'm sneaking this against orders, but "I've got a hunch"—and I wanted to write these words to you.

I've made a long voyage and been to a strange country, and I've seen the dark man very close; and I don't think I was too much afraid of him, but so much of mortality still clings to me—I wanted most desperately to live and still do, and I thought about you all a thousand times, and wanted to see you all again, and there was the impossible anguish and regret of all the work I had not done, of all the work I had to do—and I know now I'm just a grain of dust, and I feel as if a great window has been opened on life I did not know about before—and if I come through this, I hope to God I am a better man, and in some strange way I can't explain, I know I am a more deeper and a wiser one. If I get on my feet and out of here, it will be months before I head back, but if I get on my feet, I'll come back.

Whatever happens—I had this "hunch" and wanted to write you and tell you, no matter what happens or has happened, I shall always think of you and feel about you the way it was that Fourth of July day three years ago when you met me at the boat,[58] and we went out on the cafe on the river and had a drink and later went on top of the tall building, and all the strangeness and the glory and the power of life and of the city was below.

Yours always,

Tom[59]

Perhaps the best available records of the relationship between author and editor exist in the instance of F. Scott Fitzgerald in the book *Dear Scott/Dear Max*: his letters to and from his editor, Perkins, offer analysis of their relationship and in another recent book, Fitzgerald's relationship with his literary agent offers a comparison.[60] Both his editor, Perkins, and his agent, Harold Ober, served the same role and function: they were friend, counselor, advisor, literary mentor—and moneylender. Both Perkins and Ober frequently offered to lend Fitzgerald money—and he accepted. In the case of Perkins, money was lent to Fitzgerald from a running royalty account at Scribner's and, in the case of Ober, when Fitzgerald needed money, Ober's usual practice was to lend him the amount up to the expected sale of a forth-coming short story or novel.

The association between Fitzgerald and the Scribner's firm began in 1918, when, aided by the novelist, Shane Leslie, Fitzgerald submitted the manuscript of a novel tentatively titled *The Romantic Egotist*, to Scribner's. It was rejected.

Fitzgerald revised the novel and later re-submitted it to Scribner's. Three members of the editorial department read it, Perkins among them, and he voted to accept it for publication. However, he was outvoted two-to-one and was forced to return it to Fitzgerald for additional revisions and corrections. The editorial board finally accepted it for publication, and Fitzgerald became a "Perkins" author.

John Kuehl and Jackson Bryer, editors of *Dear Scott/Dear Max* write:

> The interaction between writer and editor represents the most vital aspect of this correspondence, since it goes beyond the autobiographical and demonstrates how a creative editor can affect serious writing. These letters are ideal for this purpose. Fitzgerald, who required less help than (Thomas) Wolfe yet more than (Ernest) Hemingway, received advice largely through the mail. And not only that. He had but a single publisher and editor, and his connection with them spanned two decades. Perkins' hand is everywhere.[61]

As with Thomas Wolfe, Perkins was the voice of reason and calm in his relationship with Fitzgerald, who was romantic and given to either depression or elation. In his first letter of acceptance to Fitzgerald, Perkins sets the tone of the relationship, which, by and large, he was able to maintain in the face of the author's tortured personal life, literary successes and failures and his eventual emotional bankruptcy.

Sept. 16, 1919

Dear Mr. Fitzgerald;

    I am very glad, personally, to be able to write to you that we are all for publishing your book, "This Side of Paradise." Viewing it as the same book that was here before, which in a sense it is, though translated into somewhat different terms and extended further, I think that you have improved it enormously. As the first manuscript did, it abounds in energy and life and it seems to me to be in much better proportion. I was afraid that, when we declined the first manuscript, you might be done with us conservatives. I am glad you are not. The book is so different that it is hard to prophesy how it will sell but we are all for taking a chance and supporting it with vigor....[62]

By the end of the next year, Fitzgerald was well into the habit of borrowing against royalties, as the following letter demonstrates. It must be said that Perkins in no way ever discouraged Fitzgerald in this, while the habit of borrowing against the future sales potential of his books may have contributed heavily to Fitzgerald's emotional bankruptcy in his later years.

December 2nd 1920
38 W. 59th St.

Dear Mr. Perkins:

With the settlement still over a month away I'm begging for another thousand. This will still leave me a balance of twenty-six hundred.

I've taken two weeks out to write a scenario for Dorothy Gish on order—for which I hope to get a lot of money. So it sets my novel back until Jan. 1st.

Can this nth advance be arranged?

Faithfully,[63]

The same month, Fitzgerald again had to write Perkins, with what was to become a regular litany:

38 W. 59th St.
New York City
Dec. 31, 1920

Dear Mr. Perkins:

The bank this afternoon refused to lend me anything on the security of the stock I hold—and I have been pacing the floor for an hour trying to decide what to do. Here, with the novel[64] within two weeks of completion, and I with six hundred dollars worth of bills and owing Reynolds[65] $650. for an advance on a story that I'm utterly unable to write. I've made half a dozen starts yesterday and today and I'll go mad if I have to do another debutante[66] which is what they want.

I hoped that at last being square with Scribner's I could remain so. But I'm at my wit's end. Isn't there some way you could regard this as an advance on the new novel rather than on the Xmas sale which won't be due me till July? And at the same interest that it costs Scribner's to borrow?

Or could you make it a month's loan from Scribner and Co. with my next ten books as security. I need $1600.00.

Anxiously,[67]

Yet moneylending was far from the heart of the PerkinsFitzgerald relationship. Perkins understood Fitzgerald from the beginning of their relationship, and Perkins was prepared to stand behind Fitzgerald for a long time. "We are backing you for a long race," as he phrased it in this letter to Fitzgerald after the publication of Fitzgerald's *The Beautiful and Damned*:

April 17, 1922

Dear Fitzgerald:

"*The Beautiful and Damned*" is going at about the same pace it held when you were here. It has sold about 33,000 copies actually. I doubt if we can hope it will be an overwhelming success now, but when you speak of me as being disappointed, you're wrong. I think the book has consolidated your position, so to speak,—has convinced people that as Sidney Howard says, "This Side of Paradise" was very far indeed from being all. Of course I wanted it to sell a hundred thousand or more and I hoped that the extraordinary exhilaration of your style from paragraph to paragraph might make it do so in spite of the fact that it was a tragedy and necessarily unpleasant because of its nature, so that its principal elements were not such a kind in themselves to recommend it to the very great mass of readers who read purely for entertainment and nothing else. Now, at least this book is going to have a pretty large sale. The trade are going to get rid of it easily. It has made a stir among the discriminating and has therefore been all to the good except from the most purely commercial viewpoint. I know that that is an important viewpoint to you as well as to us; but for our part we are backing you for a long race and are more than ever convinced that you will win it.

As ever,[68]

Perkins' artistic belief in Fitzgerald was very largely sustained when Fitzgerald completed the manuscript of *The Great Gatsby* in late 1924. He originally submitted it under the title *Trimalchio in West Egg* and had, at various times early in the editing process, considered the titles *Gold-Hatted Gatsby*, *On The Road to West Egg*, *Tremalchio* and *The High-bouncing Lover*. Although Perkins liked the title *Tremalchio in West Egg*, he suggested that Fitzgerald change it to *The Great Gatsby*, as he wrote to Fitzgerald in a letter of November 14, 1924:

Nov. 14, 1924

Dear Scott:

I think the novel is a wonder. I'm taking it home to read again and shall then write my impressions in full:—but it has vitality to an extraordinary degree and glamour, and a great deal of underlying thought of unusual quality. It has a kind of mystic atmosphere at times that you infused into parts of "Paradise" and have not used since. It is a marvelous fusion, into a unity of presentation, of the extraordinary incongruities of life today. And as for sheer writing, it's astonishing.

Now deal with this question: various gentlemen here don't like the title,—in fact none of them like it but me. To me, the strange incongruity of the words in it sound the note of the book. But the objectors are more practical men than I. Consider as quickly as you can the question of change.

With congratulations, I am.

Yours,[69]

Perkins later followed his first letter with a much longer one, analyzing the strengths and weaknesses of the characters and the plot and giving Fitzgerald suggestions for revisions in the manuscript.[70]

Fitzgerald hoped that the book would sell 80,000 copies, but when *The Great Gatsby* appeared in April, 1925, reviews were excellent but the book failed to capture the large audience that both Perkins and Fitzgerald hoped it would. Worse, Fitzgerald became embarrassed when literary gossip began that he might leave Scribner's for Horace Liveright, then known as a great promoter of books. Fitzgerald felt compelled to tell Perkins that he would never think of leaving Scribner's, where he had been treated so well. Fitzgerald wrote to T. R. Smith, an editor at Boni & Liveright, telling him that Scribner's was where he planned to remain. He also wrote to Perkins:

> I answered[71] at once saying that you were one of my closest friends and that my relations with Scribner's had always been so cordial and pleasant that I wouldn't think of changing publishers. That letter will reach him

at about the same time this reaches you. I have never had any other communication *of any sort* with Liveright or any other publisher except the *very definate* (sic) *and explicit letter* with which I answered their letter yesterday.[72]

Fitzgerald's career and life with Zelda slowly became a downhill slide. He was warned in late 1930 that he must never drink alcohol for a year, because his drinking was one of the reasons for Zelda's breakdown.[73]

By the mid-1930s, Perkins had to encourage and recourage Fitzgerald, whose fame rested largely on the "Jazz Age," which was being overcome and ignored by the Depression, and by the advent of newer, younger writers. In August, 1933, Perkins wrote:

August 4, 1933

Dear Scott:

When do you think I shall see you? I don't want to be away when you are likely to turn up, but I don't want to pin you down to a date, either. I hope things are going on well. You have had a mighty hard pull, but it may end rightly. Whenever any of these new writers come up who are brilliant, I always realize that you have more talent and more skill than any of them; —but circumstances have prevented you from realizing upon the fact for a long time.[74]

The next year Zelda was hospitalized in Baltimore, and again Fitzgerald was forced to borrow, or accept royalties in advance, to pay for her care.

Finally Perkins became unable to dole out money to Fitzgerald as easily as he had done in the past. The Depression made the Scribner's firm wary of extending payments and financial arrangements to Fitzgerald, a fact that Perkins had to break to Fitzgerald most discreetly.

Oct. 17, 1934

Dear Scott;

I am enclosing a royalty report because you always want to see it. We deposited the hundred, but you know, Scott, it is not quite the same here as in the old days when we had a dictatorship. We may be getting out of tune with the times, but now we have more or less of a republic. The house has half a dozen different departments, and the heads of all of them have an interest in the entire business. Charlie[75] and I understood this situation, but it is impossible to make such a one, for instance, as the head of the educational department (which, by the way, does better than we do in the depression) understand it. He would think we were just crazy, having all but cleared up your indebtedness by the way we arranged for "Tender Is the Night" to let it all pile up again. I wish to Heaven—and I know you do too—that we could work the things out some way. But you have had a run of mighty • bad luck, and have struggled against it very valiantly, and it still is true, "as the feller says" that the only sure thing about luck is that it will change.

Always yours,[76]

By the end of 1934, Fitzgerald's literary agent, Harold Ober, had to lecture him sternly because Fitzgerald was no longer reliable regarding delivery of manuscripts to magazine editors on dates due. Ober wrote:

> Up to a couple of years ago, if you had sent me word that a story would arrive on a certain date, I would have been as certain that the story would arrive as that the sun would rise the next day. Lately when you have wired me that a story would be sent on a certain date I have no faith at all that it will come.... As far as it concerns myself I do not mind this. I know life has been very difficult for you, that you have been working under pressure and that conditions that you could not help have prevented you from doing what you thought you could do....

In March, 1936, Fitzgerald wrote to Perkins, after receiving a copy of Thomas Wolfe's *Of Time and the River*, telling him how difficult it was to write and edit while drinking. Usually Fitzgerald did not mention his drinking habits to Perkins, whom he knew to be much more conservative in personal matters:

> It has become increasingly plain to me that the very excellent organization of a long book or the finest perceptions and judgment in time of revision do not go well with liquor. A short story can be written on a bottle, but for a novel you need the mental speed that enables you to keep the whole pattern in your head and ruthlessly sacrifice the sideshows as Ernest did in "A Farewell to Arms." If a mind is slowed up ever so little it lives in the individual part of a book rather than in a book as a whole; memory is dulled. I would give anything if I hadn't had to write Part III of "Tender is the Night" entirely on stimulant. If I had one more

crack at it cold sober I believe it might have made a great difference.[78]

In October, 1936, Fitzgerald received $20,000 from the estate of his mother, who had died. That money, however, meant only an immediate end to his financial problems; not a longterm solution to them as Perkins and Ober had openly hoped it would be. By the middle of 1937, Fitzgerald owed his agent, Ober, more than $12,000 which Fitzgerald had borrowed against future sales of his short stories.[79]

Only by diligent budgeting and a large salary as a script writer in Hollywood, was Fitzgerald later able to repay Ober.[80]

Despite financial setbacks and delays in writing the kinds of novels he wished to, the relationship between Fitzgerald and Perkins remained quite solid. In March, 1938, Perkins wrote Fitzgerald of how much he appreciated publishing *The Great Gatsby*, 13 years earlier.

> What a pleasure it was to publish that! It was as perfect a thing as I ever had any share in publishing.—One does not seem to get such satisfactions as that any more. Tom[81] was a kind of great adventure, but all the dreadful imperfections about him took much of the satisfaction out of it.[82]

By the middle of May, 1940, Fitzgerald was well enough along on his next novel to write to Perkins that he had completed 25,000 words. Yet the work on the novel dragged on and on, slower than he had hoped. His wife's emotional illness, his financial instability, arguments with his long-time agent Harold Ober, and his drinking habits were all hindrances to completing the novel.

Fitzgerald suffered a heart attack late in fall, 1940, and on December 21, 1940, died of a second heart attack.[83]

Although Perkins is widely known for his work with Wolfe, Fitzgerald and Hemingway, among others, there have been many other exceptional editors who worked with success and yet with less acclaim outside the book publishing business. One such editor, briefly cited earlier in this chapter, has been Cass Canfield.

Canfield, born into rather aristocratic circumstances, became associated with the house of Harper & Brothers in the early 1920s. For a time the English representative of the Harper firm, Canfield soon moved back to the United States and into the editorial mainstream with Harper's.

His first major acquisition, a fortunate accident of timing, was the work of Thornton Wilder, who chose to join the Harper firm in 1927, as a result of Canfield's suave decency, at a time when Wilder was tired of the business practices of the firm of Boni & Liveright. Canfield writes:

> My continuing association with him through the years has been a source of deep satisfaction, and I was particularly proud and pleased to publish *The Eighth Day* in 1967, forty years after the appearance of *The Bridge*. Wilder is the perfect author. Though he may take many years to finish a book, he delivers it on the date he has promised. And his manuscripts are a joy—hardly a comma needs to be changed.[84]

Shortly after Canfield's first meeting with Wilder, he was impressed enough to offer a contract to two "gloomy-looking young men" who "looked dispirited and spoke little"[85] who came with an elaborate manuscript and illustrations to the house of

Harper. The book, *Is Sex Necessary*, began the bestselling careers of James Thurber and E. B. White, of *The New Yorker* magazine.

Canfield had two of the qualities necessary for a successful editor: imagination and the ability to visualize the scope and promise of a book project. In 1936, he wrote:

> ... it occurred to me that, if I could find someone to write intimately about personalities and events in Europe, the resulting book should be useful as well as salable.[86]

Canfield commissioned a young newspaperman, John Gunther, to complete the project. Fortunately Gunther was also able to visualize the project as Canfield understood it. Gunther's book, *Inside Europe*, was, in Canfield's words:

> ... a remarkable book that was a landmark in its time and sold 150,000 copies in the original edition. Remarkable too, that anyone without a research assistant could have written a volume covering such a vast canvas.[87]

Canfield observed that Gunther's subsequent books, *Inside Asia* and *Inside Africa*, also sold well and all had the same scope and "vast canvas."

Canfield was also aware, in the late 1930s, of Thomas Wolfe's break with Maxwell Perkins and the Scribner's firm. Although reluctant to "steal" another firm's author, Canfield made inquiries and discovered that Wolfe did, indeed, wish to publish elsewhere. Canfield then arranged to have Wolfe's next books published under the Harper imprint.

As Canfield wrote:

> I got hold of him and his agent and arranged for the publication of his succeeding books. They have added much to the prestige of the Harper list; few breaks like this occur in publishing.[88]

Many a great editor makes mistakes and Canfield had not been without his own. He wrote that after George Orwell published *Down and Out in Paris and London*, "a book which didn't sell at the time of its publication but contributed to the author's reputation,"[89] Orwell's next book manuscript came to the house of Harper and to Canfield's desk. Too busy to read the manuscript, Canfield asked for a "reader's report," an analysis by a junior member of the staff. Canfield was told that the book was neither suited for children nor fit for adults, and so the manuscript was rejected. The book was Orwell's *Animal Farm* and, Canfield notes candidly..

> So we declined the manuscript—and the book has become a classic. The rejection of *Animal Farm* was disastrous, and this goof taught me to read a manuscript myself when there is the slightest question about its merit. However, occasionally a reading is impossible because the editor must make a publishing decision on the basis of an outline, sometimes on the basis of no more than a title and the author's name.[90]

Just as Perkins worked with a number of eminent authors during his career at Scribner's, so too did Canfield with a vast number of successful authors, in a wide variety of genres, during his career with Harper's. In addition to John Gunther and Thornton Wilder, Canfield's stable included Edna St. Vincent Millay (cited earlier in this chapter), Louis Bromfield, Eleanor Roosevelt, Leon Trotsky, John F. Kennedy, Eric Hoffer, Svetlana Alliluyeva and William Manchester, author of *The Death of a President*.

Unlike Perkins, who felt most at home with novelists, Canfield, who had a short career in the government during World War II, felt equally at home with political and cultural leaders, which explains, in part, his interest in authors such as Eleanor Roosevelt, John Kennedy, Svetlana Alliluyeva and Manchester and the Kennedy family again, during the publication of *The Death of a President*.

Canfield cites, in his analysis of the qualities needed to be a success as an editor, or as a publisher:

> ... the publisher needs an acquisitive instinct, although he should not let this appear on the surface. If he has an idea he believes in, or if he thinks someone can produce a first-rate book, he should continue to press for it, just short of making himself a nuisance. Often, surprisingly, a book may come into being long years after it was first discussed. The story of John Gunther's Inside Europe is an example; persistence pays off ... the publisher, who must combine the qualities of editor, gambler and businessman, should always be on the receiving end. He should take an interest in almost any subject and be content to remain anonymous, letting the author take center stage, being the creative person. The publisher, in his capacity as editor, must be the catalyst and draw people out ...[91]

While Cass Canfield was building a career which has spanned fifty years with Harper and Brothers, another editor began a career which lasted for forty-three years (1909-1952) with the Macmillan Company.

Harold S. Latham began working for Macmillan in 1909, as an office boy. Subsequently demanding (and receiving) a better position in the editorial department, Latham began a continuous rise within the company. As his responsibilities rose, so too did his editorial decisions, and negotiations with Macmillan authors.

Latham's authors, over the years of his involvement with the Macmillan Company, included Vachel Lindsay, Richard Llewellyn, H. G. Wells, Edward Arlington Robinson, and James Michener, who had worked for the Macmillan company and whom Latham was unhappy to lose. Michener, an editor in the educational department at Macmillan when he submitted his first manuscript to the editors at the trade department, was highly valued by the company. The trade department accepted his first book, *Tales of the South Pacific* and, as Latham notes:

> *Tales of the South Pacific* received excellent notices from the press, and the Pulitzer Prize. The dramatic rights were purchased by Rodgers and Hammerstein, and the highly successful musical resulted. These developments soon put the book in the list of the best sellers.[92]

The musical version of Michener's book was "South Pacific."

Soon after the publication of *Tales of the South Pacific*, the company underwent a reorganization and Michener was offered a high position in the educational department. He declined the offer to become a novelist. When the publishers expressed the idea that he "might never become a first-rate novelist,"[93] Michener thought that the statement expressed a lack of confidence in him, and he took his next book to a different firm. He however, remained a successful novelist.

Latham wrote, "the publication of (his) later books—especially *Hawaii* which I think really memorable—have fully justified his point of view. But how his Macmillan editors hated to see him go!"[94]

Cass Canfield's statement that "the publisher ... should always be on the receiving end. He should take an interest in almost any subject ..."[95] certainly applied to the author and another book with which Harold Latham has always been associated, Margaret Mitchell and *Gone With the Wind*.

In 1935, Latham journeyed to Atlanta, the first stop in a southern tour, to meet Macmillan staff members in branch offices and encourage submissions of manuscripts which might become Macmillan books, from those that were not, at that time, Macmillan authors.

Latham's contacts in Atlanta urged him to meet Mrs. Peggy Marsh, who might have a manuscript[96] worthy of publication by Macmillan. (Her maiden name was Margaret Mitchell.) At first reluctant to allow "a northerner" to read her manuscript, Mrs. Marsh agreed to let Latham have the manuscript. Latham wrote:

> The manuscript was not prepossessing; there was no first chapter; there were several final chapters. The pages were soiled, many were crumpled. But one soon forgot all this as one read. It was not many hours before I was convinced that I had something really important.[97]

The book, to be published under Mrs. Marsh's maiden name, was *Gone With the Wind*, which Latham accepted for publication by Macmillan.

Whatever its critical reputation, *Gone With the Wind* has been one of contemporary American publishing's largest selling novels. In 1965, Latham wrote:

> *Gone With the Wind* was an immediate success upon publication. Indeed, it was one of those books to which I have referred as being a success before publication. I am sure that in this case the editors of the Book-of-the-Month Club spread the news of its importance. Now, as I write, its total sales throughout the world in English and foreign-language editions, hard cover and paperback, have passed the 10,000,000 mark. Of this figure, more than one half were sold, in all editions, in the English language. The sales in translations have approximated 4,400,000. The novel has been put into Braille and on talking books for the blind. One of my prized possessions ... is a four-shelf bookcase containing nothing but translations of the story. There are over a hundred volumes in the collection with twenty-six languages represented, ranging from Japanese, Persian, Chinese, and Arabic to the more usual ones: French, German, Spanish, Italian.[98]

This type of international best-seller represents the ultimate achievement for the trade, or general editor; the successful purchase, for publication of a book which achieves international sales over a continuing basis for the company, considerable fame (and royalties) for the author and rightly, recognition within the book industry for the editor who has had the accidental good fortune or insight to accept that particular manuscript for publication. Latham has stated that any editor would have accepted the book for publication:

> I have been credited, far and wide, with having "discovered" that book.—Well, I suppose I did, if by "discovering" it one means bringing it to light; but I cannot see that this action entitles me to any special recognition. If I meet an author who has written a few pages of a work, if I read these pages and talk with the author and decide from the brief reading and the conversation that here is promise, and if I back up my confidence with a publishing contract: That, to my mind, is discovering talent. When a completed, or nearly completed, manuscript is put into my hands, and after reading it I know I have something important, something that any editor would have taken (instantly): that is not discovery; that is recognition made possible by luck. Any publisher getting his hands on *Gone With the Wind* would have "discovered" it, just as I did.[99]

However, not just "any publisher" was able to impress Mrs. Marsh with his manners and sophistication; Latham did and he received the manuscript and engineered the contract.

For those who denegate the "best seller" as something less than complete literature, Latham and others have pointed out that profits from books such as *Gone With the Wind*, which continues to sell year after year, enable Macmillan to finance other projects whose profitability seems less certain.

Latham not only published *Gone With the Wind* to co siderable continuing profit, but years earlier he also demonstrated another, facet of the editorial judgment: belief in an author whose time had not yet come. In Latham's case, editorial judgment told him that Edwin Arlington Robinson was a writer to sustain and publish. Quoting Latham:

> When Macmillan first began to publish for Mr. Robinson, his sales were pitifully small … my memory tells me that in these earlier years the maximum distribution of a new Robinson title would be well under two thousand … each work was brought out at a considerable loss.[100]

Yet Macmillan continued to publish Robinson, and he received the Pulitzer Prize in 1921 for his *Collected Poems*, received it again in 1924 for *The Man Who Died Twice* and was awarded it for the third time in 1927, for *Tristram*.[101]

Latham has contrasted the two facets of publishing: the successful popular book, exemplified by *Gone With the Wind* and sustaining belief in quality publishing, as in the case of Macmillan's long trust in the ultimate achievement and craft of Edwin Arlington Robinson.

Latham wrote:

> It is a deep satisfaction to me to recall experiences in publishing that reflect unflagging faith in the worth of an author in the face of discouraging sales. It is one thing to invest money in a perfectly creditable but completely undistinguished mystery tale, knowing full well the chances are that your investment will be returned with interest. It is quite a different matter to go on year after year promoting a writer in whom you believe and backing up your confidence with hard cash when each successive venture shows outright loss. The

one is a purely commercial deal, the other constructive and creative, adding to the dignity and meaning of publishing.[102]

Although Perkins, Canfield and Latham came to their careers in book publishing relatively early, one major figure in American contemporary book publishing entered it at what he considered a late age for beginning the business—37. Hiram Haydn had previously spent his life in teaching, first in a boy's school near Cleveland, then at the Women's College of the University of North Carolina. Haydn then began editing the magazine of the Phi Beta Kappa society, *The American Scholar*, and from there entered the book publishing industry.

Like many other editors within book publishing, Haydn moved from one company to another, as top officials changed publishing philosophies, or when Haydn himself felt a change was needed. He first began working for Nat Wartels, co-owner of Crown Publishers, and from Crown went to the editorial offices of Bobbs-Merrill, and then to Random House to work in the same offices with William Faulkner. Haydn then became co-founder, with Simon Michael Bessie and Alfred Knopf Jr., of Atheneum Publishers.

Later, in a policy dispute with Bessie and Knopf, Haydn left to become publisher of his own line of books under the Harcourt Brace Jovanovich imprint and with the encouragement of that firm's president, William Jovanovich.

In his memoirs, *Words and Faces*,[103] Haydn discusses the problems of the author-editor relationship. Quoting Haydn:

> An editor can rarely evaluate with accuracy the competence of another editor. He can form an opinion of that editor's taste and interests from the books he

acquires for his publishing house. If they are colleagues, he can appraise another's style and judgment from presentations of books at sales conferences. But the bone and sinew of editorial work are usually displayed only when writer and editor work together. How can anyone else know how much and what that editor contributes to the final shaping of the book in question?[104]

Haydn writes that editorial work on a manuscript which an author has completed includes an attempt to grasp what the author has intended in the project; where he might have fallen short of that goal or goals and the "give and take," in Haydn's words, of the revisions necessary for the book.[105]

Haydn believes that, from the point of view of British publishers, such acts of editorial judgment of the author's 'intent' are considered meddling in the author's province:

> Many British publishers and many British editors take this position. It has amused me that they, from Victor Gollancz to Fredric Warburg, have harangued me, among others, on the preposterousness of this practice, yet have owed many of their successes with books of American origin to the fidelity and patience of American editors.[106]

Haydn observes that editorial judgment and the intent of the author often make the author-editor relationship a strained one:

> It is true that an editor can, and sometimes does, meddle with a writer's work. The attempt to grasp

another's intent, and help him fulfill it, is often bumbling and presumptuous. How, in such a task, to disentangle the editor's subjective preoccupations and emotional prejudices from his inquiry into the nature of the work at hand?[107]

That answer, Haydn suggests, lies in the nature of reading; the editor must read to explore and understand the writer's meaning; of what the book *does* and how it does it. For, as Haydn writes, fulfillment for any reader must originate in a willingness to permit an invasion of his mind."[108]

What kinds of personality should editors be possessed of, to insure success in editorial work? Haydn suggests that his first love is that of exploration—in literary terms—and discovery of "the human experience" in manuscripts which cross his desk:

> ... day in and year out, his richest excitement and his surest pleasure will be instead to read a script that he finds good: strong in wisdom, illuminating of the human experience, possessed of the gift of style—that sureness with words that dazzles or satisfies through the unusual juxtaposition of the usual. I find the true editor a votary of a sort—his creed that of the word and the book.[109]

Finally, Haydn suggests, one of the strongest characteristics an editor should possess is a belief in his own judgment, his own sense of values, his own taste:

> I do not mean a fatuous egotism. Nor do I mean that any of these men is free from self-doubts and periods of

indecisiveness. But it has been my experience that able editors decide for themselves the value of a given work, aware that sometimes the consensus may go against them, but convinced that this is the only way to come to grips with a manuscript, and the only way to remain fresh in this work.[110]

Yet given all this, Haydn offers yet another suggestion about the editorial role; that of truthfulness:

> For an editor, there is another commandment equally important. Tell the truth. Forever a middleman caught between his loyalty to his authors and to his company, the editor must temper his truth-telling with some tact and some reticence. Yet better he should be blunt and even rude than a truth-shader, to say nothing of a liar. Your honest opinion about the chances of a given book, whether you are talking to its author or to your employer, is crucial.[111]

On the problems of the role of the editor in the author-editor relationship, William Jovanovich, president and chief operating officer of Harcourt Brace Jovanovich, has written:

> Editors in publishing houses are increasingly involved in the actual writing of books; they have given a pungent meaning to the old journalistic phrase "the editorial we," which stands for a common opinion that is written by a single person. Whether an editor ought to be as important as he now seems to be in the making of books is still another question, but we may be content to regard him as a necessary middleman, who in

commerce is a man who makes goods move by standing in the way.[112]

The relationship between an editor and a writer who is working in a special field creates its own problems, Jovanovich suggests, as the editor may regard the specialized author as sacrosanct, whereas his manuscript may need as much, or more copyediting and revising as a manuscript for a more general audience, or a manuscript from an author not in a specialized field:

> Editors are probably undone by embracing a double standard: they expect more of themselves than of their authors, whose writing might improve were editors less tolerant and were they to refuse to "fix" manuscripts that lack clear, spare, and engaging expression. A fallacy that all editors commit on occasion is to depend upon the professional qualifications of an author in a particular subject, to the exclusion of the question of whether he writes well.[113]

The author-editor relationship, Jovanovich believes, is a two-bladed sword. The more the author may wish his editor to help, the more dangerous the situation becomes, for where, Jovanovich asks, does help become interference?

> If a writer must borrow assistance, or merely encouragement, then it would seem natural that he turn to an editor who can be expected to be not only sympathetic but also suitably knowledgeable. For the editor this is flattering but dangerous, for he must decide at what point assistance becomes interference.[114]

Finally, Jovanovich has some hard words concerning the book publishing business as it relates to careers and job openings. Although, he believes, the trade business is more "visible" than textbook editing, it is the textbook field that offers numerically the most opportunities:

> For every editor who advises the author of a novel, there are at least twenty at work on a secondary-school science textbook. Yet the cachet of trade publishing is seemingly undiminishable. Everyone has heard of Maxwell Perkins, but who knows the name of the editor of the *Dictionary of American Biography*, of Paul A. Samuelson's *Economics*? (It is curious how Perkins as an editor has dominated the trade imagination and how little is said of his peers, among them Ben Huebsch, Pat Covici and Saxe Commins,)[115]

All of the above author-editor relationships demonstrate, at least in principle, "the best of times," the times when author and editor work together for mutual benefit and common purpose. What of the times when author and editor, or author and publishing house, seem to work in disharmony? What then?

The worst of times, in contemporary publishing history did occur to two novelists, each with the same firm, and almost at the same time.

Indiana-born Ross Lockridge Jr. began writing when he was in graduate school in English at Harvard University. Lockridge, a compulsive over-achiever, ultimately completed a manuscript which was sent to, and accepted by, Houghton Mifflin. Lockridge's work, *Raintree County*, was based loosely on the experiences and observations of distant relatives in early Indiana.

Raintree County, published by Houghton Mifflin in 1947, did phenomenally well for a first novel. It was accepted by the Book-of-the-Month Club; the film rights were sold to M.G.M. and a film planned immediately, and "escalator clauses" in Lockridge's contract with M.G.M., which promised larger profit percentages for him as sales went up, would reap great checks as the Book-of-the-Month Club and the film spurred sales of the hardcover book.

Lockridge told Martin Stone, his family lawyer, that:

> ... the book would be made into the biggest motion picture M.G.M. ever produced, would be a selection of the Book-of-the-Month Club and would win the Pulitzer Prize, thereby riding the M.G.M. escalator clauses up to the full ...[116]

Yet, Lockridge had to cut 50,000 words from the manuscript before publication, a normal editing procedure which hurt him terribly. He began a bitter dispute with the Houghton Mifflin editors on the division of profits from the motion picture rights and he began to feel, as the popularity of *Raintree County* grew and grew, that none at Houghton Mifflin cared for him; that all they wanted was great sales figures for the copies. A section of *Raintree County* was purchased by *Life* magazine and Lockridge again had to cut and trim his novel. Lockridge spent six years working on *Raintree County* and despite the fact that it was a nationwide best seller, his biographer, John Leggett, writes:

> Working on *Raintree County* had been compulsive. He was happy while doing it and miserable when not. It was the custom of six years, and moreover the discipline was lifelong. He had been trained to work at capacity

since childhood. His mother's formula, directed toward scholarship, was laced with positivism. Winning out was assumed. He had the equipment, the fine mind and sound body; all he needed was to energize them. The striving, of course, was up to him.[117]

Yet when his novel was complete, and ready for publication, he discovered he could not, or would not, leave it. The habits of the past years of his life were too strong, and he had nothing else to begin. Plans for a second novel lay incomplete and unappealing to him. Disagreements with Houghton Mifflin remained unresolved; they became an obsession which hindered all other work and further attempts at negotiations with Houghton Mifflin.

Yet, compulsively, he could not leave *Raintree County* at a time when others would have turned to a second work. Leggett writes that Lockridge was:

> ... much like a builder, his house complete, yet reluctant to leave it as he must. The house he had made of *Raintree County* was more real, to say nothing of more appealing, than the world outside and he would far rather putter around in it, even to please the fussy new tenants, than move on.[118]

Lockridge could not escape the view that his publisher, Houghton Mifflin, had not been fair to him, regarding the division of the spoils of his work, specifically the division of profits from M.G.M. He wrote an editor:

> How seriously I regard the question of ethical treatment of a young author just at the time when, because

he is neither wealthy nor established, it seems easy to put the knife in him without danger. It is just at this time that a fair and far-seeing decision on the part of the publisher is necessary to the publisher's own best interest.[119]

Soon after that letter, Lockridge's wife noticed a change in his appearance:

And yet in three months she had seen the vital, buoyant man she had loved from her girlhood turn into a man without spirit. The essence of Ross Lockridge had drained out of him as though from some hideous crack in his soul. She recognized it as the sort of collapse then euphemistically known as a nervous breakdown, but she knew that it was serious and that it was a mental as well as a physical illness.[120]

Despite all that the personnel at Houghton Mifflin could do to persuade Lockridge that he had been treated reasonably and that Houghton Mifflin was willing, at various times, to renegotiate his contracts, Lockridge felt no better about the success of *Raintree County*. He promised that because of the financial disputes with Houghton Mifflin it would never again get another manuscript from him.

Late in 1947, just before the publication of *Raintree County*, Lockridge entered the Methodist Hospital in Indianapolis for electric shock treatment for mental depression. Although he assured the doctors that the treatments were making him feel better, the reverse was actually true; he hated and feared them and they were making him worse, unable to marshal his thoughts or maintain a mental equilibrium.[121] When his book was finally published, his pre-publication income was $122,500, although taxes for the year 1947 consumed a large portion of that.

Raintree County was officially published on January 5, 1948, and Lockridge celebrated by signing copies in a hometown department store. On the evening of March 6, he got into a new Kaiser automobile he had bought from profits of his masterwork, turned on the engine, but left the automobile in his closed garage. His wife, Vernice, discovered him later, a suicide.

Before he became mentally unbalanced, he believed, firmly, that Houghton Mifflin was conspiring, with its silence or duplicity, to keep from him his fair share of the moneys, prizes and acclaim that *Raintree County* had won for him.

Another instance of intimate failure and suicide was Thomas Heggen. Like Ross Lockridge, Tom Heggen was, by birth, a mid-westerner. Born in Iowa, Heggen attended college first at Oklahoma City University, then at Oklahoma A. & M., where he majored in liberal arts and worked on the campus newspapers. When the Heggen family moved to Minneapolis, the home of Tom's mother, he transferred to the University of Minnesota, where he began working for the University newspaper, *The Daily*. Specializing in features and humor, Heggen found himself outclassed in that department by another *Daily* staff writer, who would later publish several best-selling comic novels: Max Shulman. While working on the newspapers at Oklahoma City University, A. & M. and the University of Minnesota, Heggen began writing short stories, yet nothing emerged which revealed depth of technique or style.

After graduation from Minnesota, Tom found a job with *The Reader's Digest*, which he found boring. His job was to decide which article the *Digest* might suitably print. He filed prospective articles into three piles: acceptable, passable and not acceptable. He was interested in the vast *Digest* organization, yet bored with his own small job.[122]

Heggen's career changed when the Japanese attacked Pearl Harbor. In a spirit of patriotism, he volunteered for the Navy. After several weeks on the Battleship South Dakota, Heggen requested officer training and was accepted. Heggen returned to college, this time the University of Notre Dame, in Indiana.

After officer training, Heggen was assigned to a tanker, the U.S.S. Salinas, operating in the North Atlantic. Disappointed at not receiving orders to the battle front, Heggen had to swallow his disappointment at such a boring assigmnent.[123] His assignments changed, but not his boredom: he next shipped out in the U.S.S. Agawam, another tanker, operating in the Carribbean, full of aviation gasoline.

When Heggen was assigned to the U.S.S. Virgo, his interest was piqued; the Virgo had been in action; it had carried the 3rd Marine division to the Tarawa campaign and its officers were battle veterans. The captain of the Virgo, Herbert Ezra Randall, was uniformly disliked by the officer staff, who called him "Old Stupid" behind his back. Heggen did too.[124] Inspired by the war activity aboard the Virgo, he began to write short stories about Navy life, many from his own experience, or from the experience of his friends aboard the Virgo.

He had sent copies of his war-time short stories to novelist Wallace Stegner, a distant relative, and Stegner, who had become Houghton Mifflin's West Coast editor, liked what he read. He urged that Houghton Mifflin accept Heggen's collection of stories for publication, if he would make editorial changes which would unify the stories into a complete novel. Heggen saw that his fictional junior grade officer, Doug Roberts, could indeed become the central character in his collection of related stories and he gratefully made the changes necessary for publication.[125]

At war's end, Heggen had his collection nearly complete, some of the stories had been accepted for publication in *The Atlantic Monthly*, and he had his job—if he wanted it—at *The Reader's Digest*. His bride, Carol Lynn Gilmer Heggen, had been working for *The Digest*, but yet Tom felt that returning to *The Digest* would not inspire him to further serious writing.[126]

During the late months of 1945, Tom Heggen and his wife grew farther and farther apart. His material appeared in *The Reader's Digest*, *Collier's* and *The Atlantic Monthly* and his book, now titled simply *Mister Roberts*, was due for publication in the spring of 1946. But he began to have doubts that he would find a second novel which would strike the same sparks in peacetime as *Mister Roberts* seemed to do for the war years.

Although profanity in the book made it unsuitable for the Book-of-the-Month Club, Heggen did receive a tentative offer from M.G.M. for *Mister Roberts*, which he declined. When *Mister Roberts* was published, Heggen reacted to the release with "indifferent pride," although his former classmate Max Shulman, in a review in *The Chicago Tribune*, called the book "a small masterpiece."[127]

After publication, Heggen became interested in the idea that *Mister Roberts* might be made into a dramatic play. He had seen Shulman's book, *Barefoot Boy With Cheek*, turned into a musical and he hoped that he would eventually see *Mister Roberts* on the stage.

He began working on the stage version of the adventures of Doug Roberts and his friends aboard the U.S.S. Reluctant, but could get no further than the first act. Heggen remained unable to complete the stage version of the book until he met the producer-director, Joshua Logan. Logan immediately perceived how to make Heggen's novel into a first-rate play. But slowly Heggen came to believe that the dramatic changes that Logan wanted would turn the work into something no longer his own creation. Despite his reluctance, he viewed the summer of 1947, when he was working with Logan on the play, as the best time he ever had.

After completing the playscript, Tom began working with Jo Mielziner, the set designer, on the stage setting for the play. Although the on-going activity on the play made him happy, the work at Brookfield Center, Logan's home in the suburbs, had deeply disturbed him. He began drinking and using pills to sleep, or to wake from dreamless sleep. He crested between high emotions about the play and despair that he would ever write anything creative again. He sought psychiatric help.

In February, 1948, when the novel, fashioned by Tom and Logan into a play, was first produced, it was a monumental hit. The first night production was a smash, yet he felt entirely alone, surrounded by a creation crafted by someone else. In the next day's New York newspapers, when he read of Joshua Logan's immediate plans to direct Michener's *Tales of the South Pacific*, Heggen felt betrayed. Alone except for occasional girl friends, he journeyed to Cuba, hoping to become inspired. While there, he toyed with the idea to write about a group of Flying Tiger pilots, but nothing came of it. But he and his party enjoyed talking to Ernest Hemingway, and Hemingway graciously treated Heggen as an equal—at least an equal in war experiences.

Yet Heggen's Cuban trip ended unhappily and he returned to New York to face the prospect of beginning again—and coping with the problem of what to say about peace-time which had any meaning, or any humor. The production of his play earned him several thousands of dollars per month, so much that he ceased worrying about the future.

He tried the sea again, by shipping out on a merchant seaman, the S.S. Topa Topa, but he discovered that the crew resented his presence as a passenger. The voyage did not offer him any encouragement to begin again. The success of *Mister Roberts* continued unabated; Heggen was earning eleven thousand dollars each week of the play's run.

During April, 1948, friends noticed that Heggen seemed calmer, more at peace with himself, than he had been earlier. They might not have suspected that by then he had thoughts of taking his own life, and those thoughts, his biographer believes, calmed him. The idea that he could end his own life any time he chose made the daily disappointments easier to take.

The time he chose was May 19, 1949, but he did not die like Ross Lockridge. (Late in the evening he drew a bath and took the pills he had been taking for the months previously.) A maid found him the next day and a medical examiner[128] decided the cause was "an overdose of barbiturates." He was twenty-nine years old.

Of the deaths of Ross Lockridge and Thomas Heggen, John Leggett has written:

> Success itself, even when we know it to be fantasy, holds out such promise to us all—fame, money, power and love. They are reasonable promises to the soundest minds, and the compulsion to succeed can become an obsession over which no one has control.
>
> Yet in fulfillment, success can act on a man like an hallucinogen.[129]

The careers of Lockridge and Heggen have been included here because a writer's life has a bearing on his work and cannot be separated from it; thus to analyze their author-editor relationships, we must consider their own lifestyles and, eventually, the mental and emotional maelstroms which overtook them.

The rest of this book will be an analysis of the relationship between John Steinbeck and Pascal Covici which led to the completion of Steinbeck's lasting novels and books of fact; a relationship between Steinbeck and Covici which must stand as one of contemporary American literature's most faithful and strongest author-editor combinations, for reasons which will be explained.

Chapter 1—Notes

1. He was, for many years, Dean of the Journalism School, the University of Iowa, Iowa City, and the University of Missouri, Columbia.
2. Frank Luther Mott, *Golden Multitudes* (New York: the Macmillan Co., 1947), rep. New York, The R. R. Bowker Co., n. d.
3. Ibid., pp. 285-286.
4. Ibid., p. 7.
5. Sterling G. Slappey, "Authoring Success: A Conversation with Bennett Cerf, author, wit and co-founder of Random House," in *Book Publishing: Inside Views*, Jean Spealman Kujoth, ed. (Metuchen, N. J.: The Scarecrow Press, 1971), p. 18.
6. James D. Hart, *The Popular Book, A History of America's Literary Taste* (New York: Oxford University Press, 1950), p. 285. Hart is also the author of *The Oxford Companion to American Literature*.
7. Ibid., p. 287,
8. Ibid.
9. Robert Banker, "What Makes a Book Sell?" *Publisher's Weekly*, December 4, 1954, p. 17.
10. Ibid., pp. 17-18.
11. Harold S. Latham, *My Life in Publishing* (New York: E. P. Dutton, 1965), pp. 209–210
12. Mott, *Golden Multitudes*, p. 297.
13. Cass Canfield, *Up and Down and Around. A Publisher Recollects the Time of His Life* (New York: Harper's Magazine Press, 1971), p. 206.
14. Cass Canfield, *The Publishing Experience* (Philadelphia: The University of Pennsylvania Press, 1969) , p. 10.
15. Edna St. Vincent Millay, to Cass Canfield, January 8, 1946, cited in ibid., pp. 38-39.
16. Ibid., p. 10.

17 Clifford M. Carruthers, *Ring Around Max* (DeKalb, Illinois. Northern Illinois University Press, 1973), p. xiii.
18 Ibid.
19 Ibid., p. x.
20 Maxwell E. Perkins to Ring Lardner, July 2, 1923, cited in ibid., pp. 2-3.
21 Maxwell E. Perkins to Ring Lardner, December 7, 1923, cited in ibid., pp. 4-5.
22 He was referring to F. Scott Fitzgerald.
23 Maxwell E. Perkins to Ring Lardner, February 1, 1924 cited in Carruthers, *Ring Around Max*, p. 9.
24 Perkins refers to Lardner's earlier works, which Scribner's did not publish.
25 Maxwell E. Perkins to Ring Lardner, February 18, 1924, cited in Carruthers, *Ring Around Max*, pp. 11-12.
26 Ibid., "the correspondence that follows ...," p. 2; "strongly implies ...," p. xxiii.
27 'ibid., p. x.
28 Charles A. Madison, *Irving to Irving: Author-Publisher Relations, 1800-1974* (New York: R. R. Bowker & CO., 1974), p. 198.
29 Sherwood Anderson to Trigant Burrow, October 12, 1921, cited in Howard Mumford Jones and Walter B. Rideout, *Letters of Sherwood Anderson* (Boston: Little Brown and Co., 1953), p. 74. Although Anderson speaks of his relationship with Huebsch as author and publisher, it is essentially the same as the author-editor relationship.
30 Sherwood Anderson to B. W. Huebsch, December 3, 1918, cited in Madison, *Irving to Irving*, p. 198.
31 Sherwood Anderson to Roger Sergei, December 18, 1923, cited in Jones and Rideout, *Letters of Sherwood Anderson*, p. 117.
32 B. W. Huebsch to Sherwood Anderson, n.d., cited in Madison, *Irving to Irving*, p. 199.
33 Ibid., p. 199.
34 Ibid., p. 202.
35 Ibid., p. 203.

36 Otto Liveright.
37 Sherwood Anderson to Horace Liveright, November 22, 1924, cited in Jones and Rideout, *Letters of Sherwood Anderson*, pp. 131-132.
38 It later became *Sherwood Anderson's Memoirs*.
39 Sherwood Anderson to Maxwell E. Perkins, August 10, 1933, cited in Jones and Rideout, *Letters of Sherwood Anderson*, pp. 294-295.
40 Sherwood Anderson to Maxwell E. Perkins, August 16, 1940, cited in ibid., p. 463.
41 Madison, *Irving to Irving*, p. 170.
42 Maxwell E. Perkins to Thomas Wolfe, October 22, 1928, cited in *Editor to Author, the Letters of Maxwell E. Perkins*, John Hall Wheelock, ed. (New York: Charles Scribner's Sons, 1950), p. 61.
43 Andrew Turnbull, *Thomas Wolfe* (New York: Charles Scribner's Sons, 1967), p. 126.
44 Ibid., pp. 134-135.
45 Which ultimately became *Look Homeward, Angel*.
46 Madison, *Irving to Irving*, p. 171.
47 Ibid., p. 172.
48 Ibid., p. 173.
49 Thomas Wolfe to Maxwell E. Perkins, December 24, 1929, cited in Elizabeth Nowell, ed. *The Letters of Thomas Wolfe* (New York: Charles Scribner's Sons, 1956), p. 213.
50 Maxwell E. Perkins to Thomas Wolfe, August 28, 1930, cited in *Editor to Author*, pp. 69-70.
51 Maxwell E. Perkins, cited in Madison, *Irving to Irving*, p. 175.
52 Ibid., p. 179.
53 Ibid., p. 180.
54 Maxwell E. Perkins to Thomas Wolfe, November 18, 1936, cited in *Editor to Author, The Letters of Maxwell E. Perkins*, p. 116.
55 Turnbull, *Thomas Wolfe*, p. 284.
56 Thomas Wolfe to Charles Scribner, n.d., cited in Madison, *Irving to Irving*, p. 182.
57 Perkins became Wolfe's literary executor after Wolfe's death and attended to the details of the literary estate with devotion.

58 Wolfe returned from Europe to discover that he was famous because of the publication of *Of Time and the River*.
59 Thomas Wolfe to Maxwell E. Perkins, August 12, 1938, cited in Nowell, *The Letters of Thomas Wolfe*, pp. 777–778.
60 John Kuehl and Jackson Bryer, eds. *Dear Scott/ Dear Max: The Fitzgerald-Perkins Correspondence* (New York: Charles Scribner's Sons, 1971), and Mathew J. Bruccoli, ed., *As Ever, Scott Fitz—* (Philadelphia: J. B. Lippincott Co., 1972).
61 Kuehl and Bryer, *Dear Scott/Dear Max: The Fitzgerald-Perkins Correspondence*, p. 14.
62 Maxwell E. Perkins to F. Scott Fitzgerald, September 16, 1919, cited in ibid., p. 21.
63 F. Scott Fitzgerald to Maxwell E. Perkins, December 2, 1920, cited in ibid., p. 33.
64 He was referring to *The Beautiful and Damned*.
65 Paul E. Reynolds, his first literary agent. When Harold Ober left the Reynolds agency to begin his own literary agency, Fitzgerald went with Ober.
66 He is referring to a short story with a debutante heroine.
67 F. Scott Fitzgerald to Maxwell E. Perkins, December 31, 1920, cited in Kuehl and Bryer, *Dear Scott/Dear Max: The Fitzgerald-Perkins Correspondence*, p. 34.
68 Maxwell E. Perkins to F. Scott Fitzgerald, April 17, 1922, cited in ibid., p. 58.
69 Maxwell E. Perkins to F. Scott Fitzgerald, November 14, 1924, cited in ibid., p. 82.
70 See Perkins' letter dated November 20, 1924, cited in ibid., pp. 82-84.
71 The inquiry of Boni & Liveright.
72 F. Scott Fitzgerald to Maxwell E. Perkins, June 1, 1925, cited in Kuehl and Bryer, *Dear Scott/Dear Max: The Fitzgerald-Perkins Correspondence*, p. 107.
73 See F. Scott Fitzgerald's letter to Maxwell E. Perkins, September 1, 1930, cited in ibid., pp. 169-169.
74 Maxwell E. Perkins to F. Scott Fitzgerald, August 4, 1933, cited in ibid., p. 180.

75 Charles Scribner, who had died previously.
76 Maxwell E. Perkins to F. Scott Fitzgerald, October 17, 1934, cited in Kuehl and Bryer, *Dear Scott/Dear Max: The Fitzgerald-Perkins Correspondence*, pp. 207-208.
77 Harold Ober to F. Scott Fitzgerald, December 5, 1934, cited in Bruccolli, *As Ever, Scott Fitz—*, p. 206.
78 F. Scott Fitzgerald to Maxwell E. Perkins, March 11, 1935, cited in Kuehl and Bryer, *Dear Scott/Dear Max: The Fitzgerald-Perkins Correspondence*, pp. 218-219.
79 Bruccolli, *As Ever Scott Fitz—*, p. 320.
80 See ibid., passim, pp. 319-372.
81 Thomas Wolfe, the novelist.
82 Maxwell E. Perkins to F. Scott Fitzgerald, March 9, 1938, cited in Kuehl and Bryer, *Dear Scott/Dear Max: The Fitzgerald-Perkins Correspondence*, p. 242.
83 Fitzgerald's late novel, *The Last Tycoon*, was published after his death, unfinished, with his notes about the completion he planned.
84 Canfield, *Up & Down & Around*, p. 101.
85 Ibid., p. 104.
86 Ibid., p. 121
87 Ibid., p. 123.
88 Ibid., p. 144 Canfield dismisses Aswell's role.
89 Ibid., p. 193.
90 Ibid., p. 193.
91 Ibid., p. 202.
92 Latham, *My Life in Publishing*, p. 87.
93 Ibid., p. 88
94 Ibid,. p. 89
95 Canfield, *Up & Down & Around*, pp. 202.
96 Latham, *My Life in Publishing*, p. 50.
97 Ibid.,p. 52.
98 Ibid., p. 53.
99 Ibid., p. 48.

100 Ibid..p. 43.
101 Ibid.
102 Ibid., p. 42.
103 Hiram Haydn, *Words and Faces* (New York: Harcourt Brace Jovanovich, 1974).
104 Ibid., pp. 307-308
105 Ibid., p. 308.
106 Ibid.
107 Ibid.
108 Ibid.
109 Ibid., p. 316.
110 Ibid.
111 Ibid., pp. 318-319.
112 William Jovanovich, *Now, Barabbas* (New York: Harper & Row, 1964), p. 73.
113 Ibid., p. 75.
114 Ibid., p. 80
115 Ibid., p. 18.
116 John Leggett, *Ross and Tom* (New York: Simon and Schuster, 1974), p. 130.
117 Ibid., p. 146.
118 Ibid., p. 145.
119 Ross Lockridge, n.d., cited in ibid., p. 160.
120 Ibid., p. 170.
121 Ibid., p. 190.
122 Ibid., p. 261.
123 Ibid., p. 280.
124 Ibid., p. 284.
125 Ibid., p. 296.
126 Ibid., p. 309.
127 Ibid., p. 326.
128 Ibid., p. 430.
129 Ibid., p. 433.

Chapter 2

"YOU ARE MY RAREST EXPERIENCE …"
The Careers of John Steinbeck and Pascal Covici to May, 1945

By 1945, John Steinbeck had published eleven books of fiction and non-fiction; only the last eight of these were published with Pascal Covici as editor. The first three, which were commercial failures, were published by firms which ultimately went bankrupt. Steinbeck's first novel, *Cup of Gold*, a fictionalized biography of the pirate, Henry Morgan, was published by the firm of Robert M. McBride, in New York, in 1929.[1] Lewis Gannett, the critic, wrote that his first book sold only 1,533 total copies, because few critics bothered to review it when it was published, two months after the beginning of the Great Depression.[2]

His second book, *The Pastures of Heaven*, did little better. Published during the Depression year of 1932 by the firm of Brewer, Warren & Putnam, it earned Steinbeck $400. Neither his first nor his third book earned more than the publisher's advance of $250.[3]

Although Steinbeck probably did not realize it at the time, 1933 marked the beginning of his sustained success as a professional, saleable writer. He published two short stories, which would later become parts of *The Red Pony*, and his third book, *To a God Unknown*, found a publisher, this time the firm of Robert 0. Ballou, in New York.

Before the publication of *The Pastures of Heaven*, Steinbeck had married his first wife, Carol Henning. He began the nomadic moving and settling and moving which he would continue throughout his life. Between 1930 and 1933, the Steinbecks lived in Pacific Grove, California, moved to Los Angeles and then moved again to the Monterey area, scene of his later successful novels; *Tortilla Flat*, and *The Long Valley* and near the Salinas Valley, locale of *East of Eden*.[4] For many of Steinbeck's major works, he figuratively never left the California coast, and the images of people, and places in Del Monte, Pacific Grove, Pebble Beach, Monterey, Carmel, the Corral De Terra (which became the fictional *The Pastures of Heaven*) and Salinas. Only in his later works, notably his two books written during the Second World War, *The Moon Is Down* and *Bombs Away*, and his subsequent books *The Short Reign of Pippin IV,* and *The Winter of Our Discontent* did he depart from his fictional home in the California fruit lands and small towns of his youth.

California not only furnished the locale for the best of Steinbeck's novels and short stories, but also it was in New Monterey, in 1930, that he met Ed Ricketts, a marine biologist. Ricketts and Steinbeck had heard of each other, and they immediately became great friends, a friendship which would endure until Rickett's death in an automobile-train accident in April, 1948.

Ricketts was, in many ways, as important to Steinbeck as was Pascal Covici, or Steinbeck's literary agent, Elizabeth Otis. It is generally regarded that Ricketts furnished the character for the fictional "Doc" in Steinbeck's short story, "The Snake," and the fictional character of "Doc" in *Cannery Row* and *Sweet Thursday*. Part of his personality can be seen in the character of "Doc" in *In Dubious Battle*.[5]

Ricketts also helped Steinbeck crystalize his "non-teleological" thinking; their philosophical friendship is analyzed in *John Steinbeck and Edward F. Ricketts; the shaping of a novelist*.[6]

Steinbeck and Ricketts co-authored *Sea of Cortez*[7] in 1941 and after Ricketts' untimely death, Steinbeck's lengthy and intimate portrait of Ricketts, "About Ed Ricketts," appeared in a new edition, *The Sea of Cortez: A Leisurely Journal*,[8] ten years later.

Warren French notes, "Since little attention had been paid Steinbeck's first two novels, his third. *To a God Unknown* (1933), did not impress the public of the early thirties as the surprise that it is to one who today reads the novels in the order of publication. It marked another of the 'changes of pace' for which Steinbeck was to become famous; but these changes are largely superficial, signifying not a change in the author's ideas but experiments in communicating them to a not very perceptive public.[9]

While Steinbeck's first three books were largely languishing on the bookstore shelves of mid-Depression America, he was already at work on his fourth book, *Tortilla Flat*. As he was producing that manuscript, a chance meeting in Chicago between two old friends helped change Steinbeck's career. The meeting was between a Chicago bookstore owner, Ben Abramson, and Pascal Covici, who had previously owned his own bookstore in Chicago, and later his own publishing company, Pascal Covici, Inc., Publisher. He had moved to New York to overcome the cultural disadvantages of publishing in Chicago, away from the rest of the literary world.

Covici was later described by his partner, Donald Friede, as:

> This flamboyant Roumanian with the shock of white hair on a poet's head, which in turn was set on a football player's six-foot-three body, was, is, and always will be one of the most unusual men I have ever known. We were to be associated in business for ... ten years, and almost as closely in many other ways after that, and in all that time we never once fought or had any real basic disagreement. Very probably the reason for this could be found in one of Covici's many quotations from his Roumanian grandfather. 'When two people tell you you're drunk,' Covici would quote him as saying, 'go to bed.' It was applied by him to any and all differences of opinion. And he followed his own advice and expected the people who worked with him to follow it too. The result was an effectively harmonious relationship that made life enjoyable and exciting.[10]

The results of that chance meeting between the bookstore owner and the publisher have been cited in several authoritative studies, including those by Warren French, Pascal Covici Jr. and by Peter Lisca.[11] Charles A. Madison's analysis of the Steinbeck-Covici friendship is the most detailed record extant; it appeared in Madison's *Book Publishing in America* and, in different form, in his *Irving to Irving: Author-Publisher Relationships in the U.S.*[12]

Abramson urged Covici to read *The Pastures of Heaven*, which Abramson had been remaindering; Covici did so and decided that Steinbeck was an author worth publishing. Upon returning to his New York office, Covici communicated with

Steinbeck's agent, Elizabeth Otis of the firm of McIntosh and Otis, and received Steinbeck's next manuscript, *Tortilla Flat*. It was published in 1935, a year and one-half after Steinbeck submitted it for publication to his literary agents.[14]

Because of the novel's thinly-disguised Arthurian myth-theme, or because the nation was gradually recovering from the Depression, or perhaps because of Pascal Covici's enthusiastic promotion, or a combination of all these factors, *Tortilla Flat* did well; "It appeared on the bestseller lists for several months, received the California Commonwealth Club's annual gold medal for the best novel by a California writer, was produced as a stage play, obtained for Steinbeck a Hollywood contract, and was sold to Paramount Studios."[15] For the first time in his career, John Steinbeck had money enough to relax and escape poverty. With the publication, by Covici, of *Tortilla Flat*, Steinbeck's literary foundations were set—and remained so until his death. Steinbeck remained steadfastly loyal to two who befriended him early in his career, his literary agent, Elizabeth Otis, and Covici. Despite occasional quarrels, he remained with both Otis and Covici. It is his growing relationship with Covici which is the focus of this chapter.[16]

Steinbeck's first mention of Covici occurred in a letter to a friend, George Albee, after Steinbeck had finished the manuscript of *Tortilla Flat* and while he was working on his next novel, *In Dubious Battle*. Steinbeck wrote, "I had a letter from Covici which sounded far from over-enthusiastic. I liked it. It gave me some confidence in the man. I like restraint. Covici says, 'I am interested in your work and would like to arrive at an agreement with Miss McIntosh.' My estimation of him went up immediately. It is nice to know that he is more enthusiastic than that, of course."[17]

After Covici acquired Steinbeck's *Tortilla Flat* for his publishing house, he bought the rights to Steinbeck's earlier works and began to reissue them under the Covici-Friede imprint. It was with Steinbeck's *In Dubious Battle*, however, that Covici almost lost his newly acquired author: when Steinbeck's manuscript arrived at the Covici-Friede offices, an evaluation by an editorial reader was completed, while Covici was out of the office on business. The reader rejected Steinbeck's manuscript because of what the reader analyzed as ignorance of communist labor tactics, ignoring the fact that Steinbeck's novel was *fiction*. Steinbeck was ready to turn to other publishers if Covici rejected *In Dubious Battle*. He told Mavis Macintosh to consider submitting the manuscript elsewhere if it came back from the Covici offices: "You will find a well-aroused interest in my work both at Houghton, Mifflin and at Random House."[18] Only by frantic telegrams from Covici, who discovered what had happened only when he returned to the Covici-Friede offices, was Covici able to convince Steinbeck and Elizabeth Otis that, the reader's evaluation notwithstanding, Covici *did* wish to publish *In Dubious Battle* under the Covici-Friede imprint.[19]

After the publication of *In Dubious Battle*, Steinbeck and his wife moved to Los Gatos, California. He turned to newspaper journalism and published a series of eight articles on migrant workers and their plight in California.[20] The plight of farm workers, migrant laborers and the dispossessed would remain lodged in Steinbeck's mind for four years, appearing in print in a variety of forms and styles, from *In Dubious Battle*, through "The Harvest Gypsies," and *Of Mice and Men* to *The Grapes of Wrath*, published in 1939. Selection of *Of Mice and Men* by the Book of the Month Club gave Steinbeck his first taste of real financial success and allowed him to do things which he previously had only dreams of travel and time to pursue his novels for as long as he needed.

The earliest letter from Steinbeck to Covici extant is dated February 28 (1937) and was written from Steinbeck's home in Los Gatos:

> Dear Mr. Covici:
>
> You do such nice things. The Rivera book came and I am very grateful for it. It is a valuable thing and a beautiful job. Thank you.
>
> You know, we've been married seven years or going on seven and one of the dreams of our marriage was that the moment we could, we would do some traveling. Well we're going to do it. My wife has never been on a ship. We're taking booking on a freighter sailing for New York about the first of April. We plan to go on to Europe from there. I'll give you the ship's name before we start. We haven't closed the booking yet. The boat is very slow, 31 days to N.Y.
>
> Joe Jackson told me that you had sold 117,000 copies of Mice. That's a hell of a lot of books.
>
> Anyway I'11 hope to see you before very long. You couldn't arrange to sail with us, could you train here and freighter back? That would be fine.
>
> Anyway thank you again for everything.
>
> John Steinbeck [21]

Madison writes that total sales for *Of Mice and Men* immediately after its release was "around 150,000 copies."[21]

The publishing house of Covici-Friede, during its ten-year existence, published a wide variety of genteel authors; Covici had begun his one-man operation in Chicago as publisher of art books. Covici-Friede continued this operation. As Donald Friede remembered it:

> We had started our house at the apex of the limited edition craze, and the selling of limited editions by a publisher, with good taste in content, typography, and illustrations, plus a good mailing list, was not the most difficult of problems in the summer and fall of 1928. By sacrificing taste in content, and often in illustrations as well, even better results could be obtained. Polite erotica, in editions of five to fifteen hundred copies, never stayed on the booksellers' shelves very long. They were the twentieth-century version of the library set, except that they were usually sold by means of very elaborate circulars, rather than by house-to-house canvassers. Covici had brought the art of limited-edition publishing to a high state in Chicago. Together we proceeded to improve it still further.[23]

During the existence of the Covici-Friede firm, notable publishing successes were Ben Hecht's and Charles MacArthur's *The Front Page*, Theodore Dreiser's *An American Tragedy*, Radcliffe Hall's early fictional work about lesbianism, *The Well of Loneliness*, books by e. e. cummings, and a modern version of *The Canterbury Tales* with illustrations by Rockwell Kent. Even before Steinbeck's *In Dubious Battle* and *The Grapes of Wrath*, Covici-Friede had been interested in books in the same genre. It had published successfully *Revolt Among the Sharecroppers*, *Revolt on the Campus*, *The Decline of American Capitalism* and *America Faces the Barricades*.[24]

Shortly after the publication of *Tortilla Flat* by Covici-Friede, Donald Friede, disenchanted with the publishing business, sold his shares in Covici-Friede, sub-let his apartment and journeyed west, to begin a new career as a Hollywood literary and film agent. He did, however, follow the progress of Covici-Friede, and its continuing battle with creditors, notably J. J. Little and Ives, Inc., a printing and binding company, which held notes on Covici-Friede indebtedness. As Friede remembered, in his memoirs:

> I was filled with happiness when Covici wired me that *Of Mice and Men* had been chosen by the Book-of-the-Month Club, our first book-club selection. I proudly watched it climb up on the best-seller list. I was excited by the beauty that Elmer Adler got into the limited edition of *The Red Pony*, a throwback to the day when you could still make a profit out of honestly produced books. And, in mid-1938, I felt that we safely passed the dangerous shoals, when our tenth-anniversary list announced such books as Walter Pach's *Memories,* Irving Fineman's *Doctor Adams*, new novels by Ben Hecht and Ludwig Lewisohn, a collection of short stories by John Steinbeck and promised for the spring of the following year a new novel by Steinbeck tentatively entitled *L'Affaire Lettuceburg*.[25]

But the firm of Little & Ives called its notes due: the indebtedness which had burdened Covici-Friede could not be repaid. Colonel Arthur W. Little, owner of J. J. Little & Ives, met with Covici and discussed the financial prospects of every manuscript in the hands of Covici-Friede. It was by accident that Covici had a rough proof of Steinbeck's *The Long Valley* when Colonel Little was examining the assets of Covici-Friede. As Friede remembered it:

> It was at this point that the Colonel had exploded. He produced the manuscript we had sent to Little & Ives to be set up (in type), and shook it under Covici's nose. "Look at it!" he said, pointing to the sheaf of bedraggled papers he held in his hand. 'Look at those filthy pages! It is obvious that this book has been turned down by every publisher in the country. And you dare to tell me that it will sell more than ten thousand copies!' In vain Covici tried to interrupt him, to explain that when it had been decided to publish this collection, Steinbeck had not bothered to have the manuscript retyped but had merely collected, from all the magazines that had published these stories, the original manuscripts from which they had been set. Of course they were dirty and bedraggled: compositors are not in the habit of washing their hands between pages. But the Colonel would have none of it. He had had enough, he announced. We were through. He called the creditors' meeting then and there.[26]

The firm of Covici-Friede was quickly liquidated. Friede reports that no one except himself and Pascal Covici really lost anything: every author was paid the royalties due him; creditors received full payment on past-due bills; and all office employees were able to get jobs at other publishing houses immediately after leaving the debacle of Covici-Friede.[27] As publisher Cass Canfield noted, with sympathy:

We all know of conventional publishers who have failed and whose passing evoked little regret; it is for the business failures of pioneers like Thomas Seltzer, Ben Huebsch, Pat Covici and Robert Haas that we have sympathy, for they first published writers of the stature of D. H. Lawrence, James Joyce, Thorstein Veblen, Sherwood Anderson, John Steinbeck, William Faulkner, Robert Graves and Andre Malraux.[28]

Covici joined Harold Guinzburg's The Viking Press and Steinbeck's first book under the Viking imprint was *The Long Valley*, which Colonel Little had deprecated.

It was the sudden and violent bankruptcy of Covici-Friede, however, which led to the loss of early Steinbeck-Covici papers. Only thirty-one letters and notes from Steinbeck to Covici which were written prior to 1944 are extant; one of these was cited earlier. That letter and nine others written prior to 1945 appear in the Steinbeck-Wallsten collection, *Steinbeck: A Life in Letters*. Only two letters from Covici to Steinbeck exist; neither appears in that collection. Much more material from the Covici-Friede years should exist. Donald Friede explains why it has disappeared:

> Obviously there was little we could do to stop him (Colonel Little). We—none of us–had any more money to put into the firm,[29] and besides the very calling of the meeting had given us a black eye from which it was doubtful if we could ever recover. The vultures were already swooping around, picking the titles they would like to have for their lists as soon as our corporate body was cold. But we could make sure of one thing: that no

manuscript that was not already in work would fall into Little & Ives' clutching hands. We did a good job of it too. I personally drove up to Vermont to give Fineman back the manuscript of his novel and to explain the situation to him. And Covici had a closetful of manuscripts in his apartment—safe from Colonel Little's inquiring eye.[30]

Covici's son, Dr. Pascal Covici Jr., believes that early Steinbeck-Covici correspondence may have been stored in a warehouse by his father following the foreclosure of Covici-Friede—and then lost or forgotten, or destroyed after the firm's liquidation. The correspondence which exists was sold to the University of Texas Humanities Research Center, and no other Steinbeck-Covici material is extant.[31]

Despite the unhappiness of the bankruptcy of Covici-Friede, Pascal Covici was now able to do what he did best—be an editor, and not a publisher. Friede notes that when Covici joined the staff of Harold Guinzburg's Viking Press he could "finally function as the editor he is without waking up in the morning in a cold sweat, wondering if he is going to be able to get the paper he needs without paying for the paper he has already used."[32]

Covici's son has amplified Friede's comments:

> My Father was probably the world's worst businessman. It was not just Friede who gave away money (during the Covici-Friede years); my Father did too. Both of them gave out vast royalties in advance hoping for excellent manuscripts in return. They were often disappointed, but often delighted. I think he was secretly glad to go to Viking, where he didn't have to concern himself with such matters.[33]

Covici took a calculated risk when he joined Viking he must have realized that his success with Viking was dependent upon Steinbeck's next work. *The Long Valley* did only moderately well, yet when Covici joined Viking, Steinbeck was well enough along with *The Grapes of Wrath* for the manuscript to be passed through the editorial department, after he had withdrawn *L'Affaire Lettuceburg*.

Elaine Steinbeck and Robert Wallsten described the reaction at The Viking Press after the management had read *The Grapes of Wrath* in manuscript:

> On January 9, 1939, Pascal Covici wrote Steinbeck that he, Harold Guinzburg/ President of The Viking Press, and Marshall Best, Managing Editor, had been 'emotionally exhausted after reading *The Grapes of Wrath*.' Harold Guinzburg has said "I would not change a single comma in the whole book," and Marshall Best had called it 'the most important piece of fiction on our list as he announced that the initial advertising appropriation would be $10,000. "It seemed like a kind of sacrilege to suggest revisions in so grand a book," Covici went on, but:
>
> "We felt that we would not be good publishers if we failed to point out to you any weaknesses or faults that struck us. One of these is the ending.
>
> "Your idea is to end the book on a great symbolic note, that life must go on and will go on with a greater love and sympathy and understanding for our fellowman. Nobody could fail to be moved by the incident of Rose of Sharon giving her breast to the starving man, yet, taken as the finale of such a book with all its vastness and surge, it struck us on reflection as being all

too abrupt. It seems to us that the last few pages need building up. The incident needs leading up to, so that the meeting with the starving man is not so much an accident or chance encounter, but more an integral part of the saga."

In a postscript, he added:

"Marshall has just called my attention to the fact that de Maupassant in one of his short stories 'Mid Summer Idyll' has a woman give her breast to a starving man in a railway station. Is it important?"[34]

Steinbeck's conviction about the book he had just completed is revealed in the answer he sent Covici, from his home in Los Gatos:

Los Gatos
January 16, 1939

Dear Pat:

I have your letter today. And I am sorry but I cannot change that ending. It is casual there is no fruity climax, it is not more important than any other part of the book—if there is a symbol, it is a survival symbol not a love symbol, it must be an accident, it must be a stranger, and it must be quick. To build this stranger unto the structure of the book would be to warp the whole meaning of the book. The fact that the Joads don't know him, don't care about him, have no ties with him—that is the emphasis. The giving of the breast has no more sentiment than the giving of a piece of bread. I'm sorry if that doesn't get over. It will maybe. I've been on this design and balance for a long time and I think I know how I want it. And if I'm wrong, I'm alone in my wrongness. As for the Maupassant story, I've never read it but I can't see that it makes much difference. There are no new stories and I wouldn't like them if there were. The incident of the earth mother feeding by the breast is older than literature. You know that I have never been touchy about changes, but I have too many thousands of hours on this book, every incident has been too carefully chosen and its weight judged and fitted. The balance is there. One other thing—I am not writing a satisfying story. I've done my damndest to rip a reader's nerves to rags, I don't want him satisfied.

And still one more thing—I tried to write this book the way lives are being lived not the way books are written.

This letter sounds angry. I don't mean it to be. I know that books lead to a strong deep climax. This one doesn't except by implication and the reader must bring the implication to it. If he doesn't, it wasn't a book for him to read. Throughout I've tried to make the reader participate in the actuality, what he takes from it will be scaled entirely on his own depth or hollowness. There are five layers in this book, a reader will find as many as he can and he won't find more than he has in himself.

I seem to be getting well slowly. The pain is going away. Nerves still pretty tattered but rest will stop that before too long. I fret pretty much at having to stay in bed. Guess I was pretty close to a collapse when I finally went to bed. I feel the result of it now.

Love to you all,
John[35]

It is important here, I believe, to analyze Steinbeck's statement that *The Grapes of Wrath* has "five layers" of meaning, as he has structured most of his other novels with the same layering. To my knowledge, neither Steinbeck nor any of his critics have ever analyzed his "five layers of meaning" regarding *The Grapes of Wrath*, but Antonia Siexas (Tony Ricketts), the widow of Steinbeck's friend, Ed Ricketts, found *four* layers to Steinbeck's *Of Mice and Men:*

> For Steinbeck consciously writes on several levels. A look at *Of Mice and Men* will illustrate. Three levels are apparent to the careful reader: the obvious story-level, with its tragic and to many, inexplicable ending; a 'social protest' level—and to this the great mass of readers was particularly susceptible—on which the tragedy of the rootless and helpless was portrayed with great economy and compassion by Steinbeck the reformer and a third level, apparent to the more thoughtful or imaginative—or those more inclined to read their own visions of truth into a work of art. This is the symbolic level, on which the characters can be extended to any dimension. Lennie represents the great, blind, mass-humanity, destroying out of sheer clumsiness the things it loves George represents the quick-witted, alertly shrewd shepherd and manipulator-leader. Or Lennie represents the psychological unconscious George, the conscious, and so on. The interpretations are limited only by the ingenuity of the interpreters.
>
> But there is a fourth level. The clue to it, perhaps the only clue, could have been found in the book's originally-intended title: "Something that Happened." Without

this clue, only those who know Steinbeck and knew the discussions out of which it arose could have seen the work in terms of its particular, and intended, underlying philosophy.[36]

Richard Astro's *John Steinbeck and Edward F. Ricketts: the shaping of a novelist* contains a lengthy analysis of Steinbeck's non-teleological philosophy, which in turn explains Steinbeck's original title, "Something that Happened."

Steinbeck was overwhelmed with the publicity attendant to publication of *The Grapes of Wrath*. He wrote Elizabeth Otis:

> The telegrams and telephones—all day long—speak ... speak ... speak, like hungry birds. Why the hell do people insist on speaking? the telephone is a thing of horror. And the demands for money—scholarships, memorial prizes. One man wants 47,000 dollars to buy a newspaper which will be liberal—this is supposed to run with a checkbook. Carol turned down the most absurd offer of all yesterday, to write a script in Hollywood. Carol over the telephone: 'What the hell would we do with $5,000. a week? Don't bother us!'[37]

Ultimately, the publicity and the clamor became too much for Steinbeck and his wife to handle quietly, even though his literary agents, The Viking Press, replied to some. Steinbeck was warned, candidly, that he had better watch himself, while in California, for the Associated Farmers upset by the picture Steinbeck painted in *The Grapes of Wrath*, might attempt to smear him if the opportunity presented itself Later, he wrote to Chase Horton, a family friend:

Let me tell you a story. When *The Grapes of Wrath* got loose, a lot of people were pretty mad at me. The undersheriff of Santa Clara County was a friend of mine and he told me as follows—'Don't you go into any hotel room alone. Keep records of every minute and when you are off the ranch travel with one or two friends and particularly, don't stay in a hotel alone.' 'Why?' I asked. 'Maybe I'm sticking my neck out but the boys got a rape case set up for you. You get alone in a hotel and a dame will come in, tear off her clothes, scratch her face and scream and you try to talk yourself out of that one. They won't touch your book but there's easier ways.'[38]

That, and other similar incidents, convinced Steinbeck to place records regarding inhumane treatment of migrants in locked safety deposit boxes. He also informed the FBI about the situation, and he did remain cautious when away from his home.[39]

To protect himself and his family fron continued veiled threats generated by the publication *of The Grapes of Wrath*, and to begin a new project, Steinbeck planned a trip into Mexico with Ed Ricketts. They would make a leisurely expedition through the Gulf of California, which they preferred to call by the older name, The Sea of Cortez. Although their collaboration was not published until December 5, 1941,[40] Steinbeck was planning the book as early as December 15, 1939, as seen in this letter to Elizabeth Otis:

> Now—the collecting. I got a truck and we are equipping it. We don't go to Mexico until March, but we have the handbook to do first and we'll go north in about a week I guess for the solstice tides. It will be a tough job

and I'm not at all sure we can get it done by March. And I have a terrific job of reading to do. Ricketts is all right but I am a <u>popular</u> writer and I have to build some trust in the minds of biologists. This handbook will help do that. The Mexican book will be interesting to a much larger audience, and there is no question that Viking can have it.

Yesterday we went to Berkeley with a design for our traveling refrigeration plant and it is being built. Also ordered a Bausch and Lomb SKW microscope. This is a beauty with a side bar and drum nose piece. Primarily a dissecting microscope. My dream for some time in the future is a research scope with an oil immersion lens, but that costs about 600 dollars and I'm not getting it right now. The SKW will be fine for the trip. But that research model. Oh boy! Oh boy! Sometime I'll have one. It may interest you to know that business at the lab is picking up. I can't tell you what all this means to me, in happiness and energy. I was washed up and now I'm alive again, with work to be done and worth doing.[41]

In the spring of 1940, Steinbeck won the Pulitzer Prize for fiction for *The Grapes of Wrath*. Other winners that year were Carl Sandburg, in history, for *Abraham Lincoln: The War Years*, and William Saroyan, in drama, for *The Time of Your Life*. Steinbeck's statement about the Prize was short and succinct: "While in the past I have sometimes been dubious about Pulitzer choices I am pleased and flattered to be chosen in a year when Sandburg and Saroyan were chosen. It is good, company." He later told his friend Joseph Henry Jackson that it was one of the few times "when tact and truth seem to be side by side."[42]

Still later that spring, the Steinbecks returned to Mexico where he was to write a screenplay on the life of a backward Mexican family. He was part owner of the Mexican corporation which would produce the film, "The Forgotten Village." This marked the first time Steinbeck would write for the medium of film. He later wrote the script for "Lifeboat" (1944), co-authored the script for "A Medal for Benny" (1945), and wrote "Viva Zapata!" (1950).

Late in 1940, through friends in Hollywood, Steinbeck met a singer, Gwendolyn Conger, and they became infatuated with each other. His marriage to Carol Henning was breaking up and he and Gwendolyn[43] met secretly when the occasion permitted. Steinbeck's marriage to Carol ended in divorce in early 1943.

The relationship between John Steinbeck and Pascal Covici, which previously had been cordial and mutually appreciative, began to be extremely warm and intimate. Covici worried about Steinbeck's productivity and pace, with a concern not just for a widely read and profitable author but for Steinbeck as a friend. Steinbeck, too, worked closely with Covici; he kept Covici well informed with the progress of his manuscripts, as well as his thoughts on a variety of subjects. On March 29, 1941, he wrote and asked for an advance on *Sea of Cortez*, and hoped that illustrations he and Ricketts wished to use wouldn't be prohibitively expensive:

> Monterey
> March 29, '41
>
> Dear Pat:
>
> I got your letter from the plane. Hope you were not too shocked by the request for money. But these ... illustrations are expensive and I have quite a lot in this book already. I hope you like the color plate of the shells.

I think it is beautiful. Thought perhaps you might like to print it in your prospectus. Only a suggestion. I have nearly 55,000 words of my trip narrative done and nowhere near finished. It may go as much as 80, or 90,000 thousand words and I don't care. It is a timeless job—one of the few being done in the world today—a world that is concerned with immediacies. For that reason it might have some interest if only relief to a people too raddled (*sic*) with explosives. And I think it is going to be a good job. I hope so. It will be about the only true and complete account of an expedition that I know of.

I suppose you have every reason to worry about me but when things happen by the day, sometimes they can be weathered. And that's the way they go. The word rate every day and meals and sleep. That's the way to get through.

Carol is getting back next Wednesday. She says she feels fine and healthy. I hope so. She hasn't had an easy time of it in health, as you know. I have many plans but I don't know whether any of them are feasible. This London matter becomes a little ridiculous. So many correspondents are going over that they must be cluttering up the country. Maybe I should chose some other place. Maybe Chungking or Vichy or something. One might get tromped to death by reporters in London. But if it is even reasonably possible I shall not move until this book is done. It is the last stand of sanity? and there's too damned little of it left. It seems to me a better and more important book than I had thought. But in some places it is throughly disreputable. But if it is part of the book, it goes in. And it is fun.

Mavis is not here yet. I'm anxious to see her. She will probably arrive the same time as Carol.

I guess that will be all now. Just wanted to tell you how the book was going.

John[44]

Later, Covici queried Steinbeck on the progress of the work. Steinbeck felt compelled to clarify the progress of the book and reiterate to Covici what the book *was* and what it was *not*, as Steinbeck could foresee problems with the book's merchandising. This letter was written on stationery of Ed Ricketts' Pacific Biological Laboratories, in Pacific Grove:

Pacific Grove, California
April 18

Dear Pat;

I had your letter and Ed answered most of the questions through Mavis. The main answer is to keep your shirt on. You know I won't send out second draft mss ever. [and] this less than any. Don't rush us. We're trying to do a good job and hurry [won't] help us at all. So don't sell this book until you have it. It is a huge undertaking. Another thing—this is no adventure story except as an adventure of the mind, so don't try to build up that end to your booksellers or they will just be let down. Some pictures went off to Elizabeth and she will turn them over to you for experimentation. Mostly I want you to remember that this is a scientific book. It has some general interest quite a bit in fact, but it is truly a work of science or philosophical science. What ever you wish. I'm sure you understand this and I don't want any prospective reader to be misled about it.

I hope you are well. I do about the same. My work is slowed up, I hope temporarily. But it has to come as it comes and there aren't any happy short cuts—any.

                    love to you all John.[45]

Steinbeck later wrote Bo Beskow, a friend in Sweden, about how he worked on his part of *Sea of Cortez*:

> When I wrote the text of Sea of Cortez, Gwen and I were hiding in the pine woods in a cabin and she would sleep late and I would get up and build a big fire and work until noon when she woke up and that would be the end of work for the day and we would go walking in the sand dunes and eat thousands of doughnuts and coffee. I worked very hard.[46]

The problems of his collapsing marriage to Carol, his relationship to Gwen and the completion of his book with Ed Ricketts led him to a lengthy self-analysis in a letter to Elizabeth Otis:

                    (Pacific Grove)
                    May 19, 1941
                    Monday

Dear Elizabeth;

I had your letter with the check in it a few days ago. Many thanks. I've been very [raddled] and torn out by the roots. Nightmared, etc. In many ways I have more of a sense of peace than I have ever had and am working hard but I get the horrors pretty often. It's an awful thing to me to be cruel. I don't do it well. Meanwhile, as you know, I am having my assets gone over very carefully and will give Carol half and her interest in my contracts will probably make it more. Terrific income tax this year and heavier next will cut it down of course.

I'm putting an awful burden on you. Came very close to cracking up and I guess did but not finally. Getting stronger now though. The work saves me a lot. If only Carol can be happy and whole, it will work. I don't know. I had arrived at your advice independently, not to try and think but to let the work go on and time get in some licks. Seems to be the only thing. I don't know that it is true but from her letters Carol seems more perturbed about people finding out about the separation than about the separation itself. Her terrific pride, I guess. But she is being very fine. I hope she is finding some content.

We got off a lot of draft ms. to you which you probably have by now. It is more than Pat asked for. A brutally peremptory letter from him to Ed this morning demanded it.

Don't expect any sense from me for a while or maybe never. If I can get a little work in that's all I can expect.

Meanwhile my love to all of you and don't think too badly of me—or do if it is necessary.

John[47]

A month later, he replied to a letter from Covici;
Covici had referred to Steinbeck's sub-title for *Sea of Cortez (A Leisurely Journal of Travel and Research)*, and Steinbeck discussed the philosophical content of the book. Steinbeck's wariness of critics remained high; he especially noted that Clifton Fadiman would not understand the book. This letter, too, was written on stationery of Ed Ricketts' Pacific Biological Laboratories:

Pacific Grove, California
June 19.

Dear Pat:

Good letter from you this morning which I will answer at once. I'm glad you like that subtitle. It seems with every word to define some part of the book. Personally I think there are some very funny parts in my part of it. Yesterday there was a dissertation on cannibalism and Ed today said, "Well, you have outraged every other kind of people in the world, now I think this closes the circle "and everybody will be outraged at you." It isn't bad of course, just an addenda to Swifts (*sic*) suggestion about a use for Irish babies and drawn out by the myth that the Seri Indians of Tiburon are cannibals.

We are anxious to see the jacket and the dummy. Could you send us one? We will send you as many more of the illustrations as we have right away.

Now you want to know when we think we can get the material in. I seem to see an end to my part at last. I think with two or three more good weeks I will have the first draft, barring accidents. Then the matter of second draft, another month. If you would wish to have very carefully corrected second draft rather than clear and perfect copy in a final, I could save about three weeks for you but that is for you to say. It would seem that by the first of September (*sic*), we should have it in, but there are many things which might make that impossible. I think my part should be in in august (*sic*) sometime. That's the best and nearest information I can give you. I think the book holds up. I'll be interested to see what response the salesmen find on the road, whether any interest or a lack of it. I'm pretty sure the book will be good but that doesn't mean it won't flop completely. But I do think if it gets a slow start, it will gradually pick up because there is much more than just collection in it. Gradually it will be discovered that it is a whole new approach to thinking and only very gradually will the philosophic basis emerge. Of course people like Fadiman will never know but he has kept his position not knowing things for a long time so that is not a matter to worry about. Scientific men, the good ones will know what we are talking about. In fact some of them out here already do. It will only outrage the second rate scientists, who are ready to yell mysticism the moment anything gets dangerously near to careful thinking and a little bit out of their range.

As for myself, and you say you are worrying about me. I would give up worrying. I am working as hard and as well as I can and I don't dare do anything else. I've been pretty near to a number of edges and am not away from them yet by any means but I find safety in work and that is the only safety I do find. There is no ego in my work and consequently there is no danger for me in it. All of it is extension. If it once became introverted I wouldn't last twenty-four hours. But I know that and thus am able to take care of myself. When this work is done I will have finished a cycle of work that has been "biting me for many years and it is simply the carefull (*sic*) statement of the thesis of work to be done in the future if I survive. There will be found in it hints of everything I have been driving toward and it will not be pleasant to the members of any party at all. Some one has to sit out these crises in the world and try to see them in perspective. Perhaps this book does that and perhaps it doesn't. But it does say by implication that the world will go on and that this isn't the first time.

My personal life is a curious thing which I won't permit myself to think about yet. I don't want it to get important until I have finished this work. And don't worry about my cracking up. I won't. You'll get the book and you won't be ashamed of it I don't think although you will probably be pretty much scorned and excoriated for having printed it. Because it does attack some very sacred things, but not at all viciously. Rather with good humour which may be much more devastating.

You say that you hope all will be well with me. That is a nice thing to hope although you know it won't and can't be. I haven't a hell of a lot more time but I have some. I make messes every where but I guess everyone does only with some people they don't show. So don't worry about me. I can see myself pretty objectively and the picture is a little silly

love to you all
John[48]

In a letter typical of his understanding, sympathy, and editorial support, Covici mailed Steinbeck his reply, citing Steinbeck as his "rarest experience":

July 2, 1941

Mr. John Steinbeck
Pacific Biological Laboratories
Pacific Grove, California

Dear John,

    By all means save three weeks and just give me the corrected second draft. You can make additional changes on the galleys. In fact, I believe that you will find that procedure far more convenient. It should help tremendously and save considerable time if you would mail me chapters as ready. In the interval we would carefully prepare the manuscript for the printer and shoot galleys back to you, and thus give you plenty of time to answer queries and make corrections. Please don't let anything hold this book up any longer than it is absolutely necessary. Here we are all keyed up about it, giving it a major part in our sales and advertising preparations for this year. If there is any doubt in your mind whether we will have it for this Fall, please don't wait until September to tell me; it will be too, too disappointing.

    I am sure you will get quite a variant of reviews, and I am definitely certain that "Sea of Cortez" will prove exciting, provocative and interesting to intelligent readers. This book will prove a faster seller than you think.

    I am sending you a dummy with the old title page. It will be changed for the book. I am not sending you a jacket now as some corrections are being made and will be reprinted.

    As to yourself, my worrying about you won't help I know. But I, too, see what you can give and am jealous for it. In my little life, which is about three-fourths done, you are my rarest experience. Take that with all its implications, cynically as well if you want to. The soul of man is not too simple; certainly not for me. What I do positively know is that I want you to go on. I believe most of us, as we grow older, begin to realize that somewhere, somehow things have gone wrong for us. And when one has touched life very intimately, sensitively and in humbleness one has many fears. What surprises me is that in spite of our fears we have the courage to go on.

I was hoping that your present relationship would give you the exuberance and zest for life you always wanted. I believe it has, at least to some extent, otherwise you could not go on writing. Well, as you say, we shall see.

Affectionately,
PASCAL COVICI[49]

Steinbeck replied to this letter with unusual thoughtfulness. The following letter and his previous letter dated June 19 offer a rare understanding of how and why Steinbeck was writing his share of *Sea of Cortez*. It was to continue his philosophy as previously stated ever since the publication of his first book. *Cup of Gold*:

Pacific Grove, California
July 4

Dear Pat—

I had your good letter this morning. I cannot see, Pat, any reason why this should not be there by September. I have finished my first draft and we are now doing a second like mad. I haven't talked to Ed but I think he will agree to send it as it is corrected. I'll be glad to see the dummy. I hope this is good. I (*sic*) still shaky from finishing it. It might be all right. We'll have a hundred pages, triple space typed by tomorrow and perhaps will get right to the corrections. We should be able to get out a hundred and fifty pages of this a week.

Thanks for the good thoughts. Certainly there is fulfillment here but the haunting is here too and I don't know when I will lose that. Maybe never. There are great changes in me some for the better and some, socially at least, for the worse. Word comes to me from Hollywood that I am drinking myself to death and indulging in all kinds of vices. As a matter of fact I am drinking very very little and if that other is a vice then I'm vicious. And I'm doing more work than I ever did. I love the things people say. See if the manuscript sounds like drinking. This book is very carefully planned and designed, Pat, but I don't think its plan will be immediately apparent. And again there are four levels of statement in it and I think very few will follow it down to the fourth. I even think it is a new kind of writing. I told you once that I found a great poetry in scientific writing. Perhaps I haven't done it but I've tried and it is there to be done.

I'm going to take another try at the Pipes as soon as I get a little rested—in a week or so that is. I put a hell of a lot into this ending and it pooped me a little.

Well anyway I hope you like the book. There is almost everything in it and it steps on a lot of toes. Also it is very good natured.

I guess that is all. Aren't the color pictures beautiful?

love to you all

John[50]

The key section of Steinbeck's June 19 letter is, of course:

> When this work is done I will have finished a cycle of work that has been biting me for many years and it is simply the carefull (sic) statement of the thesis of work to be done in the future if I survive. There will be found in it hints of everything I have been driving toward and it will not be pleasant to the members of any party at all.

The key section in his letter to Covici of July 4 is: "And again there are four levels of statement in it and I think very few will follow it down to the fourth."

Steinbeck never stated explicitly what his "four levels of statement" were. Peter Lisca suggests that Steinbeck has in mind "non-teleological thinking, ecology, the possible individuality of a group-animal, 'survival of the fittest,' group psyche-memory, and the mystic unity of all life. These are germinal concepts in Steinbeck …"[51]

Peter Lisca suggests that *Sea of Cortez* is as crucial to an understanding of Steinbeck as *Death in the Afternoon* and *Green Hills of Africa* are to an understanding of Hemingway's philosophy.[52]

Joseph Fontenrose examines Steinbeck's "four levels of statement" in greater detail in *John Steinbeck; An Introduction and Interpretation*, as does Freeman Champney in his essay, "John Steinbeck, Californian."[53]

Whether Covici understood Steinbeck's "four levels of statement" in *Sea of Cortez* is not certain, for there are no known letters of Covici's in existence which comment on Steinbeck's philosophy in that book.

Steinbeck finished his work on *Sea of Cortez* in August, 1941, and he and Gwen moved to the east coast. He devoted the rest of that year to beginning *The Moon Is Down*, participating in plans for the release of his film "The Forgotten Village," and negotiating for his divorce from his first wife, Carol. *Sea of Cortez* was published December 5, 1941, with an initial first printing of 7,500 copies.[54]

In one short letter to Covici, late in October, Steinbeck writes, "Started my play and it went wrong and I had to tear it down and start again. But that is normal."[55] His "play" was *The Moon Is Down*, which he conceived as both a novel *and* a play.[55]

Steinbeck later wrote to a friend how surprised he was at the acceptance of *The Moon Is Down*, after a slow sales record for *Sea of Cortez*:

> The new book is doing frighteningly well. Pre-publication it is outselling Grapes two to one. In trade edition there will be a pre-publication sale of 85,000 and Book of the Month Club is ordering 200,000. It is kind of crazy. The hysteria of the bookshops in ordering is very wild. The play is being cast now and should go into rehearsal about the 15th of February and will open about a month later.[56]

Steinbeck's next project was suggested to him by General "Hap" Arnold of the Army Air Force. General Arnold suggested that Steinbeck write a book about how bomber crews are selected, trained and sent into combat. Steinbeck liked the idea despite some bottlenecks, which Steinbeck wrote about to Covici at the end of June, 1942:

Dear Pat—

Here are some introductory pages. Look at them and see if you like them at all. The material I was promised, hasn't come from Washington and I am almost at a standstill. I suppose I'll have to learn the army game of doing nothing and passing the buck. And I don't like that game. But the Air Force set the deadline not I. If they can't get the stuff to me, there's nothing I can do about it.

Let me have that copy back. It can't even be copied until the censors are done with it.

John[57]

The Viking Press published *Bombs Away: The Story of a Bomber Team* on November 27, 1942, with a first printing of 20,000.[58]

As Lisca writes:

> The Air Force could not have chosen a better man for the job. Steinbeck's prose is straight-forward, simple, but retains some of the effectiveness of the intercalary chapters in *The Grapes of Wrath*. *Bombs Away* had a wide sale and bought by Hollywood for $250,000, but Steinbeck turned over all royalties to the Air Forces Aid Society Trust Fund. Even in such a piece of journalism as this, Steinbeck refused to compromise his integrity. The book's last chapter was to depict the climax of that rigorous training which the book describes by giving an account of an actual bombing run. Steinbeck refused to write such a chapter because he had never been on a real

bombing run and was afraid his description might be false. Instead, he ended the book very effectively with the bombers taking off for a raid …⁵⁹

Steinbeck's divorce from Carol Henning was granted March 19, 1943; on March 29, he and Gwyndolyn Conger were married in New Orleans. In early April, he became accredited as a war correspondent, working in the European Theater for The New York Herald Tribune. Steinbeck published articles in *The Herald Tribune* from the European Theater from late June, 1943, through early December.⁶⁰ Many of the pieces were collected later and published as *Once There Was a War*.

To get over the unpleasant memories of the war, the Steinbecks vacationed in Mexico, where Steinbeck learned how to sketch. He also complained about the changes in the film "Lifeboat," which had premiered, and for which he had written the script. Covici, in New York received his complaints with a greater perspective;

> And so you are learning how to draw. And like Browning's Fra Lippo Lippi
> You dream men's faces on your copy-book,
> Find eyes and nose and chin for A's and B's,
> And make a string of pictures of the world.
> Betwixt ins and outs of verb and noun.
>
> Lippi so began and why not you. And no doubt like Fra Lippo you will emerge the artist who "gives us no more of body than shows soul" and then takes breath and adds life's flash of hope, fear, sorrow or joy. I hope in your color work you prefer the most brilliant hues— the magentas, cerises, the peacock blues and Moorish yellows. What fun!

I for one don't appreciate all this fuss about "Lifeboat." The photograph (*sic*) work was extremely good and very tricky, and the acting intelligent. The story never moved me nor convinced me. I was glad when it was over—it made me a little seasick.

Right now in New York there is Spring in the air. I can almost feel the buds swell and see the purple tinge the tree trunks. Primavera is hovering over our skyline. Better come home and turn the pages with me of tomorrow.

Harold Guinzburg, as you probably know, is now in London for the O.W.I. and will shortly, perhaps, land in Italy. We shall miss him. My love to you both.

As ever
PASCAL COVICI[62]

By the summer of 1944, Steinbeck was well at work on *Cannery Row*, and he and Gwyn had moved to New York City because Gwyn was pregnant. She gave birth to their first son, Thomas, on August 2, 1944. By September, they were planning to move to the Monterey area, and then Steinbeck would travel to Mexico, from October 15 to Christmas, to write a script, to be made into the film *The Pearl*, which had been a local Mexican fable, which Steinbeck mentioned briefly in *Sea of Cortez*. But his plans changed. He bought a house in Monterey, and stayed there until after the first of 1945. In letters to Covici, Steinbeck had described his new home, "Soto House," and detailed plans for repairing and remodeling it. Covici, who was not as handy with tools as Steinbeck was, nonetheless wanted to help. With Steinbeck back in the country and settled, at least temporarily, and with *Cannery Row* about to be published, their correspondence became more frequent. During this period, Covici's letters to Steinbeck were written more often than Steinbeck could reply. In the following, Covici rejects a charge made by Carlton A. Sheffield, a long-time Steinbeck friend, that Steinbeck, with *Cannery Row*, was beginning to repeat himself:

November 15, 1944

Mr. John Steinbeck
460 Pierce Street
Monterey, Calif.

Dear John,

I should love to paint the house with you. You know how mechanically inclined I am, especially changing tires with a no good jack.

Yes, I ordered the encyclopedia and the dictionary from John Newbegin before I left. So far I haven't heard from him. I wired him today.

Here is Virginia Kirkus's comment to the trade—the booksellers throughout the country. I don't agree with your friend Sheffield. Intelligent literary critics won't say you have repeated yourself, for that doesn't mean anything. Shakespeare's "Hamlet" as well as a great many of his other characters, under different names, appear in a great many of his plays. And that doesn't make the plays less great. During the Renaissance the great painters painted the same themes over and over again and they still remain the great masterpieces of all time. I, for one, am very grateful to the spirit of your genius that when you write you never worry what the little critic will have to say.

The orders on "*Cannery Row*" are still coming in 60% higher than the "Moon is Down," and the advance on the "Moon" was 65,000 copies. We have ordered paper for 250,000 copies now and I have a feeling we will have to order more.

I am very anxious to have pictures of your house, trees, your son, Gwyn and Willie. Regards.

Yours ever,
PASCAL COVICI[63]

A week later Covici explained why the finished copies of *Cannery Row* contained no illustrations. Covici was also concerned that Steinbeck relax before tackling his next project, *The Pearl*:

> Artzybasheff could not possibly undertake to do the drawings for "*Cannery Row*." It would have been good but would not have sold additional copies. There wasn't time to experiment with other artists. I hope you don't mind too much.
>
> Yesterday I mailed you a copy of the paper edition, one of the 500 going out to the booksellers. The orders are still coming in and I am quietly excited.
>
> Now that you have baptized your new home in the name of the Father, Son and Holy Ghost—what a rambunctious ghost Gwyn would make—I hope you will take a few days off and relax completely before you start working on Pearl.
>
> Quietly soak in some ocean breezes and let your mind dwell in the depths measureless to man, then cover yourself with the hills and, the dreams will come. *The Pearl* should be pure fantasy and imagination, grounded on reality.
>
> Kindest regards.
>
> Yours ever,
> PASCAL COVICI[64]

Publication of *Cannery Row* marked the public identification of the character "Doc" as Steinbeck's friend, Ed Ricketts. Although the character of "Doc," or Ed, had been seen earlier in Steinbeck's short story, "The Snake," *Cannery Row* brought Ricketts unwanted publicity and Monterey international fame. Quoting Lisca:

> The extent to which Doc is modeled on Steinbeck's good friend, Ed Ricketts, is clear from the biographical sketch which Steinbeck published in *The Sea of Cortez: A Leisurely Journal*, after Ricketts' death. Almost every detail about Doc has its parallel in the actual life and personality of Ed Ricketts. *Cannery Row* is itself dedicated to Ed Ricketts—'For Ed Ricketts who knows why or should.' After reading the novel in manuscript, Ricketts expressed concern that it would make him a popular figure and it did. Life wanted to print photographs and a story about him and his laboratory, which Ricketts did not allow.
>
> Tourists began to drive slowly by the Pacific Biological Laboratories at 800 Oceanview Avenue. Frequently they would stop and ask if they could come in and look around.[65]

On November 30, Steinbeck wrote to Covici:

Dear Pat;
    I got a running start at this Pearl thing.
    Too fast. Had to throw the first days work away. But then it settled down. Don't know that it is any good but it moves so far and sticks together and that's all I can

expect of it. But at first I got off on the wrong foot entirely. Anyway, it is moving along and will probably pick up momentum.

Long distance phone call last night. Many from Christian Science Monitor. Wants to come down [Sunday] to discuss *Cannery Row*. Seems they have heard that I said half the whores were Christian Scientists. On the phone I said—"would you be upset if it were so? There were only two chief woman characters in the life of Jesus and one was Magdalene." "No," he said, but he wanted to discuss it. So he's coming over on Sunday and the discussion should be fun.

Maybe if I work it right we can get banned not only by Boston but by the Christian Scientists as well. The ideal is to be banned by everybody—then everybody would have to read it.[66]

After the meeting with the man from *The Christian Science Monitor*, Steinbeck wrote to Mildred Lyman, of the staff of McIntosh and Otis:

> Well, the [Xtian] Science man came and he seems very nice and cagey and clever. He 'wondered if people wouldn't get the wrong impression. I said that some people always got the wrong impression. There wasn't much he could say without giving the impression of snobbishness. When he left, he said, 'I just leave this thought with you. If they practiced prostitution and Christian Science, they were not good Christian Scientists.' And I said, 'Well, that's all right, because they weren't very good prostitutes either.' So he laughed and we parted

on a friendly basis. He said they would have to make a statement and I said I would be upset if they didn't.

The next day, Steinbeck wrote Covici that he no longer felt at ease in his own community—his successes had alienated him with the local community. Steinbeck felt they believed that *Cannery Row* had thrown their community in disrepute:

Dec. 3

Dear Pat:

The first reviews seem to bear out Sheffield's thesis exactly. But there was something he forgot. There is a time in every writer's career when the critics are gunning for him to whittle him down. This is my stage for that. It has been since *The Grapes of Wrath*. I see it all the time. The criticism is food but what saddens me is the active hatred of most of the writers and the pseudowriters around here. It will not be terribly long before we will be associating only with fishermen which is the best thing of all. There is a deep and active jealously out here that makes me very sad. I haven't mentioned it before. It is a natural reaction of course but I don't like it any the better for that.

In the same letter, he added, referring to the filming planned for *The Pearl*;

I'm still in a slump with *The Pearl*. This has been a long slump. But I have a feeling that it will never be made anyway.[68]

Covici's son has noted, "My father was usually subtle with his authors. He never said 'Do this ...'? he usually said 'This doesn't persuade me ...' I think that this subtle approach worked very well for him."[69]

From his offices, Covici worried that Steinbeck might sell his idea too quickly; that *The Pearl* might be made into a mediocre film before Steinbeck had a chance to capture all the potential which was inherent in his fable. In the following letter, he "warns" Steinbeck against this:

December 12, 1944

Mr. John Steinbeck
460 Pierce Street
Monterey, California

Dear John,

Thanks for the two snapshots of your house. What I see of it looks like an old Spanish mansion with the dust of the ages over it. The tree in the front looks magnificent. I wish I could be with you to work in the garden. Judging from the pictures I think it needs a tremendous amount of work. I know you will have fun there.

I hope you don't yield to RKO and the other movie stooges in selling your story now for a movie. At least wait until you have written . your story as you really feel it should be done. You conceived your story beautifully with poetry and a universal philosophy—all of which I am sure no movie enterprise, certainly no Hollywood studio, would even dream of reproducing on the screen. They will maim, torture and destroy what is most precious about it. I know of no reason why you should rush the story or sell it as a movie.

Harold just returned from London. He looks much better than the last time. He will stay here now and only be with the OWI part of the time. He asked about you and Gwyn and your son. He is very happy with the wonderful advance of *Cannery Row*.

The slow recovery of Gwyn doesn't sound very good to me. What does the doctor say? I know your contempt for doctors.

Love,[70]

The next week, with the official publication date of *Cannery Row* approaching, Covici sent Steinbeck further details of the book's publication. This letter also suggests the intimacy which Covici wished with his favorite author. With Steinbeck living on the west coast and Covici in New York, they could breakfast together only in Covici's imagination:

December 19, 1944

Mr. John Steinbeck
460 Pierce Street
Monterey, Calif.

Dear John,

No, I haven't received your report of the Christian Science interview. Please let me have it. I am sure it's too good to miss.

"*Cannery Row*" will be published on January 2nd. Judging from the orders already in I would say that the advance will be between 90,000 and 95,000. If you remember the advance on *"The Moon Is Down"* was 65,000 in spite of the book club selection. Our total sales of the "Moon" was about 165,000 copies. I am still willing to stick my neck out and say that *"Cannery Row"* will sell not less than 250,000 copies. We shall see.

You are surely beginning to enjoy your son. It wasn't until he was about nine months old when I really began to notice Pascal. From then on he was fun.

I should be there when you start out for your office, meet you casually and go for breakfast. What will you have? Yes, let's have coffee first, lots of it. Orange juice? No. Let's have some Persian melon this morning, ham and eggs, please, for two, rye toast, and please have it well done, almost burned. We like it burned. Do you think they will give it to us burned? Probably not. The coffee is good here, is it not? Very good.

Well, now that we have had breakfast you can start to work.

Love,[71]

Cannery Row was officially published on January 2, 1945, with a first printing of 78,000.[72]

On December 29, Steinbeck wrote a typical letter to Covici; however, in this letter he discusses the problems of sustained creativity:

I've gone into a slump on the Pearl and that bothers me even remembering that I always go into two or three slumps on every book. But it always worries me.

You know you can inspect my slumps pretty well. I go grey in the head and then I begin to worry about not working. Then I get disgusted with myself and when this disgust grows big enough the whole thing turns over like an iceberg and I go to work again. It's always the same and it's always new. I never get used to it.[73]

After the first of the year, Covici encouraged Steinbeck to forget the criticism of *Cannery Row*, forget the pre-Christmas problems with the Christian Scientists, and stop worrying about his writer's slumps:

January 8, 1945

Mr. John Steinbeck
460 Pierce Street
Monterey, California

Dear John,

Reorders are already coming in. The American News Co. received 20,000 copies last week, the initial order, and they called up today for 2500 more. Smaller shops who originally ordered 25 and 50 are wiring in for duplications.

The small fry of writers and some of the academic ones will always be gunning for you. Were you to be merely a successful writer, like~Fannie Hurst, Temple Bailey or Dr. Cronin, you would be occasionally patronized in an oily way but mostly ignored. But to be successful and command serious critical attention—that's too much. They can't stomach it and so they will take it out on you no matter what you write. Better start building a tougher protective skin around you.

Poisonous javelins will be constantly coming your way. Make good use of your philosophic calm and demeanor, even against your friends. They, too, are human and frailty, thy name is human.

Why don't you leave Pearl rest a while and to hell with deadlines? You shouldn't whip yourself into work. It just isn't any good. San Francisco should give you some respite. I should be with you now drinking wine and listening to some old Roumanian songs, grow sad and mellow and warm inside. That's a very good feeling to have.

Love,[74]

A generation later, publisher William Targ has noted:

It is essential that an editor and publishing executive remember his *humanness*....

The author and his manuscript are the most important elements in your professional life. Let the author know this. Everything you do, every action you undertake should be with this in mind....

Treat the author with every possible courtesy; remember he's palpitating from blood-drain, from the efforts expended on his book, and needs encouragement and friendship.

Your author must know in his heart that you are always leveling with him. If you don't like something, tell him/her; if you are pleased, speak up. Your author must trust you ...[75]

Covici's letters to Steinbeck exhibit the qualities of humanness which Targ later suggested were so important in the professional life of the publisher. Covici had, at his best, a perceptive understanding for his treatment of his authors.

In Steinbeck's case, his relationship was far beyond that of author and publisher, to that of a spirited, concerned intimacy, concerned with Steinbeck's physical and emotional health, as well as his professional career. In the middle of January, 1945, Steinbeck wrote to Covici, again saying that he didn't believe that the critics had discovered the structure of *Cannery Row;*

> ... It is interesting to me, Pat, that no critic .has discovered the reason for these little chapters in C. R. You would have known. Nearly all lay readers know. Only critics don't. Are they somehow the lowest common denominator. If in pictures, the thing must be slanted for the 9 year old mind, in books they must be slanted for critics and it seems to amount to the same thing. Far from being the sharpest readers, they are the dullest. You say I am taking it philosophically. I'm not and I feel wonderful. Don't you remember the years when these same critics were sneering at every book—the same books incidentially that they now remember with awe. No, I feel all of the old contempt for them and it is a good feeling. I <u>know</u> C.R. is a good book.[76]

On January 18, 1945, Covici wrote, "If the reviews make you feel full of hell and arouse your energy they have done a remarkable deed.... It is a good mood to begin anything in—I mean full of hell."

He also noted, in that same letter, "I have just been informed that the Book-of-the-Month Club selected your *Red Pony Illustrated* for a dividend book this year. In shiny dollars that means a minimum of $16,000. for you."[77]

The next week, he felt compelled to write:

> I read "*Cannery Row*" over again. It's a good book, John. You poured a great deal of poetry into it. You give a good many reasons for living and for dying. And I am glad you were born and happy that you are alive. Certainly life is an accident. Man is no more important to the Universe than an ant on the Sahara Desert. But we are important to each other—we are born in each other's image.[78]

Later that spring, Steinbeck wrote to Covici of his ever-increasing belief that he could not live in Monterey, where all his former friends had turned against him:

Dear Pat:

This is a private letter really. We're going to Mexico in a few days. And I'm glad to go. You remember how happy I was to come back here. It really was a home coming. Well there is no home coming nor any welcome. What there is is jealousy and hatred and the knife in the back. I'm beginning to think I made a mistake. I don't mind that but I'm not going to let a mistake ride me on through. This is no new thing. I've tried to conceal it and explain it and analyze it and make a joke of it and to ignore it. It's much more than a feeling.

Our old friends won't have us back—always except Ed. Mostly with them it is what they consider success that gets in between. And the town and the region—that is the people of it—just pure poison. I laughed about being refused an office. But the local gas board cut off my gas in spite of the fact that I had a job with the War Food Administration. Ours is the first request to repair a house that has been rejected. 60 homes are being built for rent but we can't get a plank to replace a rotten board in the kitchen. These are just two of many things. I hate a feeling of persecution but I am just not welcome here.

But I'm not going to jump any guns. We're going to be in Mexico four or five months and then we'll give it another try and if it doesn't work we'll clear out.

Maybe you can figure something, but this I can tell you, I was happier in New York. Living is people, not places. I have no peers here—in notoriety and so called success and the people who are coming up are ferocious. There's no one to talk to except Ed. You see, Pat—I would and can forget all the publicity etc. but these people can't and won't.

This isn't my country anymore. And it won't be until I am dead. It makes me very sad.

John[79]

Before Covici could reply, Steinbeck moved to Mexico. Covici's answer was mailed to him there, in care of the company which was producing the film, *The Pearl*.

April 10, 1945

Mr. John Steinbeck
Aquila Films
Ejido 43
Mexico, D.F., Mexico

Dear John,

    Your letter made me very sad. I expected a different homecoming When you bought your house, the home you really wanted, I was glad and very hopeful for your happiness. This small town stuff never occurred to me. Thinking it over, as I have done for the last few days, I believe I understand quite clearly why you feel that way. New York is a big metropolis of many races and nationalities where big reputations are made and lost almost daily, where poverty and riches change hands almost hourly. One more reputation, one more success is quickly swallowed. You lived in New York long enough to hate the provincialism of a small town, their jealousies and hatreds. You are a real success, one of their boys who tops them all; tops them too much for their comfort. You have a national reputation and came home to enjoy it and I am afraid they won't let you. There are plenty of the same calibre in New York but you don't have to see them nor be with them. You can choose your friends here and plenty to choose from. One can live in an apartment here for years and not know one's next door neighbor. Not so in a small town. Either they take you in or you are forever an outsider.

    The combined provincial hostilities of the town pitted against you is tragic to contemplate. There is a certain voiceless, lacerating malice in small town inhabitants that can be deadly poisonous. They have no loyalties except for their own of equal stature. Of course, try it again when you return. But as you say, living is people not places and New York has both. You have a great many friends here, and I am afraid that destiny has something else in store for you.

"There's a divinity that shapes our ends,
Rough-hew them how we will ..."
Maybe so.

Affectionately yours,[80]

As the Steinbeck-Covici relationship grew stronger, Covici occasionally had to explain Steinbeck's perceptions, needs and problems in a way Steinbeck himself could understand. This letter above is one of the first in which Covici, as a master psychologist, must explain Steinbeck's own choices and thoughts to him.

Steinbeck, who had first written about the fable of the "Pearl of the World" in *Sea of Cortez*, now finished his book-length treatment of that story and had forwarded it to Covici, for publication. Covici replied as soon as he could comparing it to *The Grapes of Wrath* in excellence:

April 26, 1945

Mr. John Steinbeck
Hotel Reforma
Mexico, D.F., Mexico

Dear John,

I just finished "La Perla" and I like it. To me it is as tense and compelling a story as I have read in years. in this parade you say there are only black and white things and no in-between, but what rich blacks and what dazzling whites. The love of Juana for Kino is quite elemental, but with the strength and vividness of all things elemental. Kino's exulting response to the song of the family which runs through your story like a light motif, a distant and insistent beat of a tomtom, is also primitive and elemental but it is eternal in the heart of man. One could also say about your parable that, like Juana's song to Coyotito, it has only three notes—love, hunger and freedom from greed. But again what infinite longings you put into them.

This undoubtedly contains some of your best prose. The scorpion passage and the one where you tell of the trackers pursuing Kino, his breathless escapes, his final plunge in the dark and his knifing the man are, to my mind, the most intense, exciting, compulsive prose you have ever written.

If this sounds over-bubbling I can't help it. It is what I feel.

Affectionately,[82]

Later Covici wrote again, sketching in possibilities of combining *The Pearl* with other of Steinbeck's works to make a larger volume. Eventually, *The Pearl* was published separately, but this letter is indicative of how a good editor evaluates all possibilities for an in-coming manuscript.

May 7, 1945

Mr. John Steinbeck
Hotel Marik
Cuernavaca, Morelos, Mexico

Dear John,

After I talked to Elizabeth Otis I was convinced more than ever that *The Pearl* should be published either in a limited edition similar to the first issue of "The Red Pony" or, and that would delight me most, to wait until you have two more similar stories and then bring out a volume of three novelettes of Mexico. So published the book would not only receive serious critical attention, but I believe it would have a very good sale. What's far more interesting, a volume of short novels would be so completely different than anything you have published. What do you think? Couldn't the new Mexican story you now have in mind be one of them? Then that Good Neighbor story which you never finished. Don't you think that you could do something with it? The first half I thought was superb. Anyway, let me know how you feel about all this.

I could use a bit of Mexico, and to be there with you and Gwyn would be a wishful dream fulfilled, but there isn't a ghost of a chance of my coming now. By the time this letter reaches you the war with Germany will undoubtedly be over and then what? Chaos for the next hundred years or a new dawn? Your guess is as good as mine.[83]

The years 1945 to 1952 offer a panoramic view of Steinbeck; his career and his relationship to Covici. This period reveals Steinbeck at his best; from *The Pearl* and *The Wayward Bus*, through the book which critics generally agree was his worst, *Burning Bright*, and then on to the work he considered his magnum opus, *East of Eden*. These years reveal Steinbeck happily married to Gwyn Conger, then sadness during their divorce, then happiness again when he meets and marries Elaine Scott.

Throughout these years, the support of Pascal Covici, his editorial and personal friendship and guidance continues, culminating in the dedication of Steinbeck's *East of Eden* to Covici, and the collection and eventual publication of *Journal of a Novel; The East of Eden Letters*, which were all written to Covici during the progress of *East of Eden*.

Chapter 2—Notes

1. The first three Steinbeck novels are generally not considered in the top tier in the Steinbeck canon.
2. Lewis Gannett, cited in Warren French, *John Steinbeck* (New York: Twayne Publishers, 1961), p. 21.
3. French, *John Steinbeck*, pp. 21-22.
4. Elaine Steinbeck and Robert Wallsten, *Steinbeck: A Life in Letters* (New York: The Viking Press, 1975) contains maps indicating the locations of Steinbeck's homes in California.
5. French, *John Steinbeck*, pp. 21-22. Nelson Valjean believes that Steinbeck used Ricketts' character "in six novels, depicting him as Friend (Ed) in *Burning Bright*, as Doc in *Cannery Row*, Doc Burton in *In Dubious Battle*, Jim Casy in *The Grapes of Wrath*, Doc Winter in *The Moon Is Down* and Doc in Sweet Thursday." Nelson Valjean, *John Steinbeck: Errant Knight* (San Francisco: Chronicle Books, 1975), p. 135.
6. Richard Astro, *John Steinbeck and Edward F. Ricketts: the shaping of a novelist* (Minneapolis: The University of Minnesota Press, 1973).
7. John Steinbeck and Edward F. Ricketts, *Sea of Cortez: A Leisurely Journal of Travel and Research* (New York: The Viking Press, 1941).
8. John Steinbeck, *The Sea of Cortez: A Leisurely Journal* (New York: The Viking Press, 1951).
9. French, *John Steinbeck*, p. 47.
10. Donald Friede, *The Mechanical Angel* (New York: Alfred Knopf, 1948), p. 80. This volume, now out-of-print, describes the partnership of Covici and Friede during the years of the Covici-Friede Company, including a brief mention of John Steinbeck's acceptance by the firm. A large percentage of the book details Friede's career as a west coast agent after the Covici-Friede firm

went bankrupt. A portion of *The Mechanical Angel* which deals with the Covici-Friede Company is excerpted in *Publishers on Publishing*, ed. by Gerald Gross (New York: R. R. Bowker Co. and Grosset & Dunlap, 1961), pp. 326-353. Pascal Covici says that his Father was five feet, ten and one-half inches tall, not six feet three, as Friede says. Letter to author 5 January 1977.

11 French, *John Steinbeck*, p. 23; The Portable Steinbeck, revised, selected and introduced by Pascal Covici, Jr. (New York: The Viking Press, 1971), p. xxxiii, and Peter Lisca, *The Wide World of John Steinbeck* (New Brunswick, New Jersey: Rutgers University Press, 1958), pp. 74-75.

12 Charles A. Madison, *Book Publishing in America* (New York: McGraw-Hill, 1966), pp. 305-309, and Irving to Irving, Author-Publisher Relationship 1800-1974 (New York: R. R. Bowker, 1975), pp. 205-212.

13 John Steinbeck, *Tortilla Flat* (New York: Covici-Friede, 1935).

14 Lisca, *The Wide World of John Steinbeck*, p. 75.

15 Ibid.

16 It is not the province of this study to analyze Steinbeck's novels; critical studies of Steinbeck's work are listed in the Bibliography.

17 Letter from John Steinbeck to George Albee, dated only "1935" in Steinbeck and Wallsten, *Steinbeck: A Life in Letters*, pp. 101-102. Early in his career, his work was handled by Mavis Macintosh, but Steinbeck's work was turned over to Elizabeth Otis, and it was she who remained Steinbeck's literary agent.

18 Ibid., p. 107.

19 For a detailed analysis of this period, see Ibid., pp. 107-110.

20 John Steinbeck, "The Harvest Gypsies," *San Francisco News*, 5 October-12 October 1936.

21 John Steinbeck to Pascal Covici, Los Gatos, 28 February 1937. Humanities Research Center, University of Texas, Austin. (Hereafter abbreviated as UTHRC.) Covici had sent Steinbeck a copy of a recently published book by the artist, Diego Rivera. Joe Jackson was Joseph Henry Jackson, book reviewer for The San Francisco Chronicle, who had previously reviewed *In Dubious Battle*.

22 Madison, *Book Publishing in America*, p. 306.
23 Friede, *The Mechanical Angel*, p. 84.
24 Friede's *The Mechanical Angel* contains a summary of the publishing practices of Covici-Friede prior to Covici's discovery of John Steinbeck: passim, pp. 83-121.
25 Ibid., p. 129.
26 Ibid., p. 131.
27 Friede's view of the collapse of Covici-Friede is contained in *The Mechanical Angel*, pp. 122-133.
28 Canfield, *Up & Down & Around:*, p. 203.
29 He refers to the firm of Covici-Friede.
30 Friede, *The Mechanical Angel*, p. 131.
31 Dr. Pascal Covici, Jr., Interview at Southern Methodist University, Dallas, Texas, 19 December 1975. Dr. Covici and other Steinbeck scholars have searched for additional Steinbeck-Covici materials and none save the University of Texas collection has ever been found. Thus, the author of this study has examined all Steinbeck-Covici materials known to exist.
32 Friede, *The Mechanical Angel*, p. 132.
33 Pascal Covici, Jr., Interview at Southern Methodist University.
34 Steinbeck and Wallsten, *Steinbeck: A Life in Letters*, p. 177.
35 John Steinbeck to Pascal Covici, 16 January 1939. UTHRC. Steinbeck did, eventually, change the last scene as the editors at Viking wished him to. Marshall Best said, in an interview in his home, in Sharon, Connecticut, December 1, 1975, thirty-six years after *The Grapes of Wrath* was published that "everyone was terribly excited about it," when the manuscript reached the Viking offices. "One of our readers noticed that Steinbeck had the girl—Rose of Sharon—offering her breast to the starving man too soon after her baby was born, stillborn and blue. We pointed this out to Steinbeck and he made a change in that last scene—he lengthened it to make the act physiologically possible." Marshall Best could remember the smallest details from *The Grapes of Wrath*, although he did not re-read it for the interview.

Steinbeck's statement "The pain is going away. Nerves still pretty tattered but rest will stop that before too long ..." was in reference to a dislodged vertebra and general exhaustion following the completion of *The Grapes of Wrath*.

36   Antonia Seixas, "John Steinbeck and the Non-teleological Bus," in *Steinbeck and His Critics: A Record of Twenty-Five Years*, ed. E. W. Tedlock, Jr. and C. V. Wicker (Albuquerque: The University of New Mexico Press, 1957), pp. 276-277.

37   Steinbeck and Wallsten, *Steinbeck: A Life in Letters*, p. 183. Steinbeck's anguish over his flood of personal publicity can be seen in his letters to friends, pp. 178-196.

38   Ibid., p. 187.

39   Ibid.

40   Michele Medinz, Copyright Department, The Viking Press, letter, 10 October 1975.

41   Steinbeck and Wallsten, *Steinbeck: A Life in Letters*, pp. 196-197. Steinbeck and Ricketts were planning a short guidebook to the coastal waters north of San Francisco, as a warm-up to Sea of Cortez. Steinbeck's reference to "business at the lab is picking up" referred to Ricketts' Pacific Biological Laboratories, in Pacific Grove, California. Steinbeck would later disguise it in *Cannery Row* and *Sweet Thursday* as "Western Biological Laboratory." The trip to Mexico for Sea of Cortez was made during late March and April, 1940.

42   Steinbeck and Wallsten, *Steinbeck: A Life in Letters*, p. 205.

43   The break-up of Steinbeck's first marriage and his marriage to Gwyn Conger are seen in ibid., passim, pp. 213–251. A confusion has grown up in Steinbeck criticism about her genealogy. In *John Steinbeck* (1961), Warren French notes in a chronology: "1943: Married Gwyn Verdon" p. 16, apparently confusing her with the Broadway star, Gwen Verdon. The mistake was repeated by Pascal Covici, Jr., in his Introduction and Chronology to *The Portable Steinbeck* (1971), and elsewhere. Steinbeck's second wife's last name was Conger, and she was not the star Gwen Verdon. Pascal Covici, Jr. admitted his mistake and described Warren French's in an interview at Southern Methodist University, Dallas, 19 December 1975.

44   John Steinbeck to Pascal Covici, 29 March 1941, UTHRC. Steinbeck had long-range plans to be accredited as a war

correspondent in the European Theater, which, at that time, was a favorite locale for the adventuresome. He feared too many reporters might already be covering the war from England. Mavis Macintosh, one of the women in his literary agency, Macintosh & Otis, was planning a visit, about the same time his wife, Carol, was returning from a vacation.

45 John Steinbeck to Pascal Covici, 18 April 1941, UTHRC. Throughout his career, Elizabeth Otis, as his agent, was often sent sections of completed manuscripts before Steinbeck sent them to Covici, or to Viking Press. In this instance, Steinbeck forwarded sections of the illustrations to Covici, through Elizabeth Otis.

46 Steinbeck and Wallsten, *Steinbeck: A Life in Letters*, p. 228.

47 Ibid., p. 229. Steinbeck and others often referred to Pascal Covici as "Pat."

48 John Steinbeck to Pascal Covici, 18 June 1941, UTHRC.

49 Pascal Covici to John Steinbeck, 2 July 1941, UTHRC. All Covici's letters to Steinbeck were written from Covici's New York Viking Press offices. For convenience and to save space in this study, Covici's office address has been omitted from the top of all his letters.

50 John Steinbeck to Pascal Covici, 4 July 1941, UTHRC. Steinbeck's reference to "and if that other is a vice than I'm vicious" apparently refers to Hollywood gossip about his extramarital affair with Gwen Conger. Steinbeck and Wallsten in *Steinbeck: A Life in Letters* have translated Steinbeck's handwriting in his letter as "I told you once that I found a great paltry in scientific writing." In view of Steinbeck's attempt to resolve his own philosophy through the medium of his handwriting as "I have found a great poetry in scientific writing" to be the correct interpretation. Lisca translates the same passage as "I have found a great poetry ..." (p. 181). Steinbeck's reference to "the Pipes" was to a piece of fiction which he never completed.

51 Lisca, *The Wide World of John Steinbeck*, p. 181. Lisca discusses the development of Sea of Cortez, pp. 178-184.

52 Ibid., p. 183.

53 Joseph Fontenrose, John Steinbeck: An Introduction and Interpretation (New York: Holt, Rinehart and Winston, Inc.,

1963), pp. 84-97. That section was also reprinted as "Sea of Cortez" in Steinbeck: A Collection of Critical Essays, ed. by Robert Murray Davis (Englewood Cliffs, New Jersey: Prentice-Hall, Inc., 1972), pp. 122-134. Freeman Champney, "John Steinbeck, Californian," in Steinbeck and His Critics, pp. 135-151.

54 Michele Medinz, Copyright Department, The Viking Press, letter, 10 October 1975.

55 John Steinbeck to Pascal Covici (no date—annotated 'read 10/27/41'), UTHRC.

56 John Steinbeck to Webster F. Street in Steinbeck and Wallsten, *Steinbeck: A Life in Letters*, p. 242. *The Moon Is Down* was published March 6, 1942, with a first printing of 55,000 copies. The Dramatist Guild published it in play form August 11, 1942 and The Viking Press also published a play form September 25, 1942, with a first edition of 250. Michele Medinz, Copyright Department, The Viking Press, letter 10 October 1975. During this period, Gwendolyn Conger changed the spelling of her first name to "Gwyndolyn" and it will be spelled that way hereafter.

57 John Steinbeck to Pascal Covici (no date; annotated 'read 6/30/52'), UTHRC.

58 Michele Medinz, Copyright Department, The Viking Press, letter, 10 October 1975.

59 Lisca, *The Wide World of John Steinbeck*, pp. 184-195.

60 Tetsumaro Hayashi, *A New Steinbeck Bibliography* (Metuchen, New Jersey: The Scarecrow Press, 1973), pp. 15-16.

61 John Steinbeck, *Once There Was a War* (New York: The Viking Press, 1958).

62 Pascal Covici to John Steinbeck, 25 February 1944, UTHRC. Harold Guinsburg, the president of The Viking Press, had been in London, working for the Office of War Information.

63 Pascal Covici to John Steinbeck, 15 November 1944, UTHRC. Covici's reference to "I ordered the encyclopedia and the dictionary ..." were part of a long-standing custom with the two. If Steinbeck found a book in a catalogue which he needed, Covici would order it, and usually get it at a discount, at The Viking Press. Covici would then mail it on to Steinbeck and charge the cost of the book or books against Steinbeck's earned royalties.

Covici's feelings were that this type of errand was the least that he could do for his busy friend—there is no evidence that he ever passed the jobs off to secretaries or other staff members. Willie was the current Steinbeck dog.

64 Pascal Covici to John Steinbeck, 22 November 1944, UTHRC.

65 Lisca, *The Wide World of John Steinbeck*, pp. 213-214. Critical analyses of *Cannery Row* can be found in the titles listed in the Bibliography, at the end of this study.

66 John Steinbeck to Pascal Covici, 30 November 1944, UTHRC.

67 John Steinbeck to Mildred Lyman, in Steinbeck and Wallsten, *Steinbeck: A Life in Letters*, pp. 276-277. The dialogue between Steinbeck and representatives of the Christian Science Church went on throughout the month of December. Representatives of the Christian Science Church visited Pascal Covici in his Viking Press offices, but *Cannery Row* was not changed in any way. Steinbeck viewed their concern as needless meddling in his novel; Covici, who viewed the dialogue at a great distance and with less involvement, cherished the whole matter as an amusing anecdote.

68 John Steinbeck to Pascal Covici, 3 December 1944, UTHRC

69 Dr. Pascal Covici, Jr. Interview at Southern Methodist University, Dallas, Texas, 19 December 1975.

70 Pascal Covici to John Steinbeck, 12 December 1944, UTHRC. The Viking Press only held the rights to publish Steinbeck's work in book form in the U.S.; film rights, magazine rights and overseas publication rights were held by Steinbeck's agents, thus the right to sell *The Pearl* to a Hollywood film company could be negotiated by Macintosh and Otis, with Steinbeck's approval, without the approval of Covici or The Viking Press. This is usual literary agency policy.

71 Pascal Covici to John Steinbeck, 19 December 1944, UTHRC.

72 Michele Medinz, Copyright Department, The Viking Press, letter, 10 October 1975.

73 John Steinbeck to Pascal Covici, 29 December 1944, UTHRC.

74 Pascal Covici to John Steinbeck, 8 January 1945, UTHRC. Many of the later Covici letters to Steinbeck were unsigned; thus Covici's signature will be deleted.

75 William Targ, *Indecent Pleasures* (New York: Macmillan, 1975), pp. 251-252.
76 John Steinbeck to Pascal Covici, 15 January 1945, UTHRC.
77 Pascal Covici to John Steinbeck, 18 January 1945, UTHRC.
78 Pascal Covici to John Steinbeck, 25 January 1945, UTHRC.
79 John Steinbeck to Pascal Covici (no date-—spring, 1945, from Monterey), UTHRC.
80 Pascal Covici to John Steinbeck, 10 April 1945, UTHRC.
81 Steinbeck and Ricketts, Sea of Cortez, pp. 102–103
82 Pascal Covici to John Steinbeck, 26 April 1945, Covici mailed this to Steinbeck's hotel in Mexico.
83 Pascal Covici to John Steinbeck, 7 May 1945, UTHRC.

Index

Abraham Lincoln: The War Years, 93
Abramson, Ben, 77
Adler, Elmer, 83
Albee, George, 79
Alliluyeva, Svetlana, 47
Amazon, ii–iii
American Crisis, 4
America Faces the Barricades, 82
American Scholar, The, 53
An American Tragedy, 82
Anderson, Sherwood, 17, 18, 19, 21–22, 23, 24–25
And To Think That I Saw It on Mulberry Street, v
Animal Farm, 46
Arnold, Gen. Hap, 106
Artyzabasheff, Boris, 111
Astro, Richard, 91
Aswell, Edward, 31–32
Atlantic Monthly, 6
Atheneum Publishers, 53

Bailey, Temple, 118
Ballou, Robert, 76
Banker, Robert, 6
Barefoot Boy with Cheek, 64
Beautiful and the Damned, The, 37
Bernstein, Aline, 25

Bertelsmann, i
Bessie, Simon Michael, 53
Best, Marshall, 88
Bezos, Jeff, ii
Book of the Month Club, ii. 6–7, 50, 59, 64 80, 83, 123
Bombs Away, 76
Boners, v
Boni And Liveright, 25, 39
Book Publishing in America, 78
Brewer, Warren and Putnam, 75
Bridge, The, 44
Bromfield, Louis, 47
Bryer, Jackson, 34
Burning Bright, 127

Canfield, Cass, 8–9, 11, 44–45, 46, 47, 48, 53, 84–85
Capote, Truman, 4
Cannery Row, 109–110, 111–112, 113, 116, 118, 120
Caruthers, Clifford M, 12
Case of the Curious Bride, The, 5
Cat in the Hat, The, vi
Cerf, Bennett, v–vi, 3–4
Chapney, Freeman, 105
Chicago Tribune, The, 64
Collected Poems, 62
Colliers, 64
Commins, Saxe, 58
Cosmopolitan, 12, 15
Covici, Pascal, iv–v, 58, 67, 75–127
Covici, Pascal Jr. 78, 86, 115
Covici-Friede, iv, 81–86, 126

Crown Publishers, 53
Cummings, e.e, 82
Carruthers, Clifford, 12, 17
Cup of Gold, 75, 103

Dark Laughter, 20
Dear Scott / Dear Max, 33–34
Death of a President, The, 47
DeVoto, Bernard, 30
Dickens, Charles, 1
Dictionary of American Biography, The, 58
Doctor Adams, 83
Doubleday, 31
Doubleday Book Stores, 6
Down and Out in Paris and London, 46
Dreiser, Theodor, 82
Dr. Seuss, v–vi
Durant, Will, 4

East of Eden, 76, 127
Economics, 58
Eighth Day, The, 44

Fadiman, Clifton, 98, 100
Faulkner, William, 53, 85
Fineman, Irving, 83
Fitzgerald F. Scott, 12, 13, 14, 25, 35, 36–37, 39–40, 41, 42–43 44
Fitzgerald, Zelda, 40
500 Hats of Bartholomew Cubbins, The, v
Forgotten Village, The, 94
Fontenrore, Joseph, 105

French, Warren, 78
Friede, Donald, 78, 82, 83, 95–96
Front Page, The, 82

Gardner, Erle Stanley, 5
Geisel, Theodor, v–vi
Golden Multitudes, 23
Gollancz, Victor, 54
Gone with the Wind, 49–50
Graves, Robert, 85
Grapes of Wrath, The, v, 87, 88–89, 91, 107, 114, 124
Great Gatsby The, 38–39, 43
Green Eggs and Ham, vi
Green Hills of Africa, 105
Guinzburg, Harold, 109, 116
Gunther, John. 45–47

Hackette Group, ii
Hall, Radcliffe, 82
Harcourt Brace, 26
Harcourt Brace Jovanovich, 53
Harper Collins, ii
Harper's, 44, 45
Hart, James D., 4–5
"Harvest Gypsies, The," 80
Haydn, Hiram, 53–54, 55–56
Hecht, Ben, 82, 83
Heggen, Carol, 64
Heggen, Tom, 62, 63, 64, 66, 67
Hemingway, Ernest, 12, 14, 34, 44, 65
Henry Holt Co., 17

Hills Beyond, The, 32
Hoffer, Eric., 47
Horton Chase, 91
Houghton Mifflin, 31, 59, 60, 61, 63
Huebsch, B.W., 18–19, 20, 24, 58, 85
In Dubious Battle, 79–80
Inside Africa, 45
Inside Asia, 45
Inside Europe, 56, 47
Is Sex Necessary? 45
Irving to Irving, 78

Jackson, Joseph Henry, 93
J.J. Little and Ives Co., 83
John Steinbeck: An Introduction and Interpretation, 105
John Steinbeck and E. F. Ricketts; The shaping of a novelist, 91
Joyce, James, 85
Jovanovich, William, 53, 56–58
Journal of a Novel: The East of Eden Letters, 127

Kodansha, ii
Kennedy, John, 47
Kent, Rockwell, 82
King's Stilts, The, v
Knopf, Alfred Jr., 53
Kuehl, John 34

L'Affaire Lettuceburg, 83
Lardner, Ring, 11–17
Latham, Harold, 6, 48, 51–53
Lawrence, D.H., 85

Leggett, John, 59–60, 61, 66
Leslie, Shane, 34
Lewisohn, Ludwig, 83
Lifeboat, 94, 108
Life, 59
Lightning Source, iii–iv
Lindsay, Vachel, 48
Lisca, Peter, 78, 105
Little, Arthur, 83
Liveright, Horace, 20–21, 24, 39
Llewellyn, Richard 48
Lockridge, Ross, 58–62, 66, 67
Logan, Joshua, 65
Long Valley, The, 76
Look Homeward, Angel, 28, 31

MacArthur, Charles, 82
MacIntosh, Mavis, 80
Macmillan, ii, 48
Madison, Charles, 17, 27–28, 78
Man Who Was Dr. Seuss, The, v
Man Who Died Twice, The, 52
Manchester, William, 47
McClure's, 12, 15
McGraw-Hill, ii
Medal for Benny, A, 94
Memories, 83
MGM, 59, 64
Michener, James, 4, 48–49
Mielziner, Jo, 65
Millay, Edna St. Vincent, 9–11, 47

Mister Roberts, 64
Mitchell, Margaret, 49
Modern Library, 19
Moon Is Down, The, 106

New York Herald Tribune, The, 108

Ober, Harold, 33–34, 41–42, 43
O'Hara, John, 4
Of Mice and Men, 80, 81, 83, 90–91
One Fish Two Fish Red Fish Blue Fish, v
Of Time and the River, 30, 42
Once There Was a River, 108
Orwell, George, 46
Otis, Elizabeth, 76, 79, 91, 92–93, 126

Pach, Walter, 83
Paine, Thomas, 4
Pan, Florence, ii
Paramount Studios, 79
Pastures of Heaven, The, 75, 78
Pearl, The, 109, 114, 115, 122, 124–125, 126
Pearson Publishing, Co., 1
Penguin-Random House, i, ii
Perkins, Maxwell, 12, 13, 14–16, 22–23, 24,, 26, 27, 28, 29, 30–31, 35, 37–38, 39–40, 41, 43, 45, 53, 58
Print on Demand Publishing, i–ii

Raintree County, 58, 59–60, 61, 62
Random House, 53
Reader's Digest, 62, 64

Red Pony, The, 76, 83
Red Pony Illustrated, The, 126
Revolt on the Campus, 82
Revolt Among the Sharecroppers, 82
RKO Studios, 115
Ricketts, Ed., 76–77, 92, 12, 12
Robert M. McBride Co., 75
Robinson, Edward Arlington, 48, 52
Rodgers and Hammerstein, 48
Romantic Egoist, The, 34
Ronsley, Jill, iii
Roosevelt Eleanor, 47

Samuelson, Paul, 58
Sayoran, William, 43
Scribner Charles, 31–32
Scribner's, 26
Saturday Evening Post, The, 12, 15
Sea of Cortez, 77, 94–95, 97, 98, 102, 106, 109, 112, 124
Scholastic, ii
Shuman, Max, 62, 64
Seven Lady Godivas, v
Sherwood Anderson's Memoirs, 24
Smith T.R, 39
Springer Nature, ii
Stegner, Wallace, 63
Steinbeck, Carol, 76, 94–96, 97
Steinbeck, Elaine, 87
Steinbeck Gwen, 94, 97
Steinbeck, John, iv–v, 67, 75–127
Steinbeck and Covici: The Story of a Friendship, v

Story of a Novel, The, 30
Story of Philosophy, The, 4
Story Tellers Story, A, 21, 23
Stowe, Harriet Beecher, 4

Tales of the South Pacific, 48–65
Time of Your Life, The, 13
Turnbull, Andrew, 26–27
Thurber, James, 45
To a God Unkown, 76
Tortilla Flat, 76, 79, 80
Tristam, 52
Trotsky, Leon, 47

Uncle Tom's Cabin, 4

Vanguard Press, v–vi
Veblen, Throsten, 55
Viking Press, iv, 86
Viva Zapata, 94

Wallsten, Robert, 87

Bibliography

Astro, Richard. *John Steinbeck and Edward F. Ricketts: The Shaping of a Novelist*. Minneapolis: The University of Minnesota Press, 1973.

Banker, Robert. "What Makes a Book Sell?" *Publisher's Weekly*, Dec. 4, 1954.

Bruccoli, Mathew J., ed., *As Ever, Scott Fitz —* New York: Lippincott, 1972.

Canfield, Cass. *Up and Down and Around: A Publisher Recollects the Time of His Life*. New York: Harper's Magazine Press, 1971.

Carruthers, Clifford. *Ring Around Max*. DeKalb, HI.: Northern Illinois University Press, 1973.

Davis, Robert Murray. *Steinbeck: A Collection of Critical Essays*. Englewood Cliffs, N. J.: Prentice-Hall, 1972.

Fensch, Thomas. *Steinbeck and Covici; The Story of a Friendship*. Middlebury, Vt: Paul S. Eriksson, 1979. Reprint ed. New Century Books, 2002 .

Fontenrose, Joseph. *John Steinbeck: An Introduction and Interpretation*. New York: Holt, Rinehart and Winston, 1963.

French, Warren. *John Steinbeck*. New York: Twayne Publishers, 1961.

Fensch, Thomas. *The Man Who Was Dr. Seuss: The Life and Work of Theodor Geisel*. N. Chesterfield, Va.: New Century Books, 2000.

_____. *Steinbeck and Covici: The Story of a Friendship*. Middlebury, Vt., Paul S. Eriksson, Publisher, 1979. Reprint ed. New Century Books, 2002

_____. *The Portable Steinbeck*. New York: The Viking Press, 1971.

Friede, Donald. *The Mechanical Angel.* New York: Alfred Knopf, 1948.

Gross, Gerald. *Publishers on Publishing.* New York: R.R. Bowker, 1961.

Harris, Elizabeth A. and Alexandra Alter. "A Big Publishing Merger Was Blocked, but Brought the Industry Little Clarity." *The New York Times*, Nov. 1, 2022 .

Hart, James. D. *The Popular Book: A History of America's Literary Taste.* New York: Oxford University Press, 1950.

Hayashi, Tetsumaro. *A New Steinbeck Bibliography.* Metuchen, N.J.: The Scarecrow Press, 1973.

Haydn, Hiram. *Words and Faces.* New York: Harcourt Brace Jovanovich, 1974.

Jones, Howard Mumford and Walter B. Rideout. *Letters of Sherwood Anderson.* Boston: Little Brown, 1953.

Jovanovich, William. *Now, Barabbas.* New York: Harper and Row, 1964.

Kuehl, John and Jackson Bryer, eds. *Dear Scott/Dear Max: The Fitzgerald-Perkins Correspondence.* New York: Charles Scribner's Sons, 1971.

Kujoth, Jean Spealman, *Book Publishing: Inside Views.* Metuchen, N.J.: Scarecrow Press, 1950.

Latham, Harold S. *My Life in Publishing.* New York: E.P. Dutton, 1965.

Leggett, John. *Ross and Tom.* New York: Simon and Schuster, 1974.

Lisca, Peter. *The Wide World of John Steinbeck.* New Brunswick, N.J.: Rutgers University Press, 1958.

Madison, Charles A. *Book Publishing in America.* New York: McGraw-Hill, 1965.

_____. *Irving to Irving: Author-Publisher Relations, 1800-1974.* New York: R.R. Bowker Co., 1974.

Mazur, Caitlin. "The 15 Largest Publishing Companies in the World." zippa.com website, April 18, 2023.

Mott, Prank Luther. *Golden Multitudes.* New York: Macmillan, 1947.

Nowell, Elizabeth ed., *The Letters of Thomas Wolfe.* New York: Charles Scribner's Sons, 1956.

Steinbeck, Elaine and Robert Wallsten. *Steinbeck; A Life in Letters.* New York: The Viking Press, 1975.

Steinbeck, John. "The Harvest Gypsies." *The San Francisco News,* 5 October–12 October, 1936.

_____. *The Sea of Cortez: A Leisurely Journal.* New York: The Viking Press, 1951.

_____. *Once There Was a War.* New York: The Viking Press, 1958.

Steinbeck John and Edward P. Ricketts. *Sea of Cortez: A Leisurely Journal of Travel and Research.* New York: The Viking Press, 1951.

Targ, William. *Indecent Pleasures.* New York: Macmillan, 1975.

Tedlock, E.W. and C.V. Wicker. *Steinbeck and His Critics: A Record of Twenty-Five Years.* Albequerque: The University of New Mexico Press, 1957.

Wheelock, John Hall. *Editor to Author: The Letters of Maxwell E. Perkins.* New York: Charles Scribner's Sons, 1950.

About the Author

THOMAS FENSCH began publishing books in 1970; he is now the author of 47 books of nonfiction.

His 1979 book, *Steinbeck and Covici: The Story of a Friendship*, was the first analysis of the relationship between John Steinbeck and his editor-publisher Pascal Covici. It was highly reviewed in *The New York Times* and widely reviewed elsewhere, and has long been considered a seminal work in Steinbeck scholarship; it has been continuously in print since 1979. He has published four other books on Steinbeck.

He contributed a lengthy Introduction to the latest paperback edition of *Tortilla Flat*.

He is also the principal biographer of John Howard Griffin, who dyed his skin black and toured the south in the pre-Civil Rights days of the late 1950s. Griffin published *Black Like Me* which became—and still is—an American classic.

Fensch's biography, *The Man Who Changed His Skin: The Life and Work of John Howard Griffin* was published in 2011.

He has a doctorate in print communication from Syracuse University and lives outside Richmond, Va., with a posse of dogs, his senior literary advisors, who are always ready to fetch yellow pencils, legal pads and the like.

www.ingramcontent.com/pod-product-compliance
Lightning Source LLC
LaVergne TN
LVHW010216070526
838199LV00062B/4620